Realizzazione editoriale e testi
Edizioni del Baldo

Traduzione
Elisabetta Orlandi

Illustrazioni
Francesca Mazzini, Selene Conti,
Giulia Pianigiani, Laura Toffaletti e Mario Stoppele

Grafica e impaginazione
Edizioni del Baldo

ITALIAN COOKING

I edizione settembre 2013
© Edizioni del Baldo

© Edizioni del Baldo
Via M.G. Agnesi, 49
37014 Castelnuovo del Garda - Verona
Tel 045 8960275 Fax 045 4852084
info@pizzighella.com
Visita il nostro sito:
www.edizionidelbaldo.it

ITALIAN COOKING

Flavour of food on the Italian roads

RISOTTO

RIBOLLITA

PANE CARASAU

PIZZA

ORECCHIETTE

TORTELLINI

130 recipes
of the most important Italian regional tradition

Index of regions of Italy

Sicily	5
Sardinia	16
Calabria	24
Puglia	32
Campania	38
Abruzzo	46
Lazio	52
Umbria	64
Marche	66
Tuscany	72
Emilia Romagna	86
Liguria	101
Piedmont - Aosta Valley	111
Lombardy	120
Veneto	130
Trentino Alto Adige Südtirol	148
Friuli Venezia Giulia	154

SPAGHETTI alla NORMA

360 g spaghetti, 1 big aubergine,
500 g ripe tomatoes, 2 cloves garlic,
a few basil leaves, 50 g all-purpose
flour, 1 teaspoon sugar,
50 g grated mature ricotta cheese
(or pecorino cheese), extra-virgin
olive oil, salt.

Clean and trim the aubergine, cut it into slices about ½ cm thick. Sprinkle the slices with coarse salt, lay into a drainer and cover with a plate. Leave for one hour to eliminate the bitter juices. Rinse, dry well and fry in hot olive oil. Leave to dry on paper towels. Put aside a few slices and cut the others into sticks. In a saucepan, fry the crushed garlic in four tablespoons of olive oil, add the peeled and chopped tomatoes, a pinch of salt and the sugar. Simmer for about 20 minutes over moderate heat. Pass the sauce through a sieve and then put it back over the heat, adding the aubergine and the crushed basil. Leave to thicken for about 20 minutes. Boil the spaghetti in plenty of hot salted water, drain when al dente and transfer to a serving bowl. Mix with the tomato sauce, sprinkle with the grated ricotta and decorate with the slices of aubergine previously put aside.

This is a classic Italian recipe from the city of Catania in Sicily. It was so named to honor the successful opera "Norma" of the Sicilia composer Vincenzo Bettini.

360 g bucatini, 400 g fresh sardines, 2 small bunches wild fennel (or 1 teaspoon fennel seeds, or ½ teaspoon tamaro, which is a mixture of spices: coriander, fennel, star anise, anise, cinnamon), 1 large onion, 1 tablespoon raisins, 1 tablespoon pine nuts, 5 anchovy fillets, 2 tablespoons breadcrumbs, extra-virgin olive oil, 1 sachet saffron, salt.

Soak the raisins in lukewarm water for 15 minutes. Boil the wild fennel (just the hearts) in plenty of hot salted water, drain and thinly chop but keep the water on the side (later on you will use it to boil the pasta). Instead of wild fennel you can spice the water by using fennel seeds or *tamaro* (in a little fabric sachet), which have to be added upfront to the cooking water. Clean and bone the sardines, discard heads, fins and entrails, rinse and leave to dry. Sauté the finely chopped onion and the anchovy fillets in a pan with olive oil. Add the sardines and sauté for a few minutes over moderate heat. Add the boiled fennel, the raisins (drained), the pine nuts and the saffron, diluted in half a glass of water. Season with salt and simmer over low heat for about ten minutes. Boil the *bucatini* in plenty of hot salted water, drain when al dente and pour in the pan containing the sauce. Sauté for a couple of minutes, stirring well. Sprinkle with breadcrumbs, previously sautéed in some olive oil, and serve.

Bucatini with sardines and fennel

Bucatini is a thick spaghetti-like pasta with a hole running through the center. The name "buco" in Italian means "hole".

Arancini di riso

(Sicilian stuffed fried rice balls, so called because they are similar to little oranges)

For the arancini (little oranges): 500 g rice, 50 g butter, ¼ l milk, 2 tablespoons grated Parmesan cheese, 4 eggs, nutmeg, 100 g all-purpose flour, 100 g breadcrumbs, salt.
For the filling: 2 spoonful Bolognese sauce, 50 g peas (you can use frozen peas), 100 scamorza cheese (or fresh provola cheese).
Peanut oil for deep frying.

Prepare a thick version of Bolognese sauce, then boil the peas and add them to the sauce. Cube the scamorza cheese. Put on the stove a pot of water (1 ¼ l), add the milk, two pinches of salt, the butter and a pinch of nutmeg. When it starts boiling, add the rice and cook over moderate heat, stirring carefully. When all the liquid has been absorbed, stir for another 15 minutes and remove from heat. Add two egg yolks (keep the egg whites aside) and the Parmesan cheese. Mix well all the ingredients, pour into a bowl and leave the mixture to cool down. Take a big tablespoon of rice and use your hands to mould it into a ball the size of a little orange. Make a hole with your finger and stuff the ball with the Bolognese sauce filling and a couple of cheese cubes, then close the hole. Leave the *arancini* to firm up for about 15 minutes, then coat them with flour, dip them into the beaten eggs (2 eggs plus the egg whites you put aside) and the bread-crumbs. Brown them evenly in hot olive oil, drain and serve hot.

Sauté the onion and the garlic (previously peeled and sliced) in a pan with four tablespoons of olive oil, add the chopped tomatoes (or the tomato pulp), a pinch of sugar (to reduce acidity) and a pinch of salt. Simmer over moderate heat, partially covered by a lid, for about 30 minutes. Remove from the heat; if you used fresh tomatoes pass the sauce through a sieve. Add some crushed basil leaves. Peel and trim the aubergines: by peeling them you will get rid of the bitter juices, mainly contained in the skin. Cut the aubergines into slices about ½ cm thick, quickly dip the slices into slightly salted olive oil and grill them on both sides until lightly charred. If you want the *Parmigiana* to be tastier, dip the aubergine slices in flour and fry them in hot olive oil. Lightly grease a baking dish (medium size, about 22x30 cm; in case you don't have one, a disposable aluminum tray will do) and spread with a layer of tomato sauce. Arrange a layer of sliced aubergines (pack them tightly), pour over some tomato sauce, sprinkle with Parmesan, then arrange a layer of mozzarella slices and a layer of mortadella. Repeat the layers until you have used up all the ingredients. Finish with a layer of sauce and sprinkle with Parmesan. Garnish with some basil leaves and bake for about 30-40 minutes in a pre-heated oven (200 °C), until slightly browned. Allow to cool and serve. In Summer, the aubergine *Parmigiana* can be served cold.

4 large aubergines, 400 g mozzarella cheese (or caciocavallo cheese), 150 sliced mortadella, 1 onion, 1 clove garlic, 1 kg ripe tomatoes, (or 750 g tomato pulp), basil, 80 g grated Parmesan cheese, sugar, extra-virgin olive oil, salt.

Aubergine
PARMIGIANA

Parmigiana does not mean, as usually, "from Parma", but evidences the use of Parmesan cheese.

Aubergine Caponata

(Sicilian style ratatouille)

2 large aubergines, 2 onions, ½ kg ripe tomatoes,
50 g green olives (pitted), 1 tablespoon capers,
1 celery stalk, 1 teaspoon sugar, extra-virgin olive oil,
½ glass vinegar, salt.

Plunge the tomatoes in boiling water for a minute, cool under running water, peel them, remove the seeds and stalks and chop into tiny cubes. Peel the aubergines, dice them and simmer in a pan with a little olive oil and a pinch of salt. When the aubergines begin to colour, remove from the heat.
Brown the thinly sliced onions in a pan with some olive oil, add the diced tomatoes and then the crushed olives, the capers and the sliced celery. Season with salt, lower the heat and cover the pan. Continue cooking for about 10 minutes, then add the aubergines and stir. Continue cooking for a further five minutes. Add the sugar, previously dissolved in vinegar, stir and cook over a high heat, uncovered, until the sauce gets thicker. Serve warm or, better, cold.

4 artichokes, 4 oil-packed anchovy fillets, 100 g breadcrumbs, 40 g grated pecorino cheese, 1 small bunch parsley, 1 tablespoon capers, 1 clove garlic, extra-virgin olive oil, salt.

Wash and clean the artichokes: remove the tough outer leaves and cut off the tops and the stems so that each artichoke can be placed in the pan. Using your fingertips, open up all the leaves - starting from the outer leaves and reaching the core of the artichoke - so they can be stuffed. Crush the anchovy fillets, chop the parsley, the capers and crush the garlic. Mix well all these ingredients with the breadcrumbs and the pecorino cheese, then season with salt, place the stuffing between the loosened leaves and drizzle with olive oil. Arrange the artichokes standing upright in a casserole with a little olive oil. Place a funnel between the artichokes and the side of the casserole and pour enough slightly salted water to cover the artichokes half way. Simmer over low heat covering the casserole with a lid. Check frequently, to make sure there's always enough water in the casserole (add some hot water if necessary). After about 30 minutes uncover and leave to cook for a further five minutes. Artichokes are done when, pulling a leaf, it comes off easily. Arrange the artichokes on a serving dish and eat them picking the leaves one by one, with their stuffing. Pull off one leaf, starting at the base of the artichoke. Then hold the leaf between your thumb and your index and drawn the base of the leaf between your clenched teeth, to scrape off the soft portion and the stuffing, discarding the rest of the leaf. A real treat!

"Alla messinese" means Messina style. Messina is one of the beautiful city the island of Sicily

Stuffed artichokes "alla messinese"

Roast kid with potatoes

800 g kid meat, 600 g potatoes,
2 onions, 2 cloves garlic, 4 ripe tomatoes,
1 sprig rosemary, 3 or 4 sage leaves, 10 basil leaves,
1 glass dry white wine, 1 glass vinegar,
extra-virgin olive oil, salt, pepper.

Clean and chop the kid meat, place in a large bowl and leave to marinate for a couple of hours in abundant water - aromatized with vinegar, crushed sage leaves and a sprig of rosemary - in order to tone down the gamey flavour and odour of the meat.

Drain the meat, dry the kid chops and place them in an oiled oven-proof dish. Add the potatoes (previously peeled and chopped), the crushed garlic, the tomatoes (peeled and cut into two halves), the chopped onions, the basil leaves (crushed). Sprinkle with wine and olive oil, add salt and pepper and cook in a pre-heated oven (180 °C) for an hour. Turn the meat and the potatoes over every so often, basting them with the cooking juices and adding wine or hot water if needed. Once cooked, turn off the oven and leave the meat in for a few minutes. Meat and potatoes must be dry but tender. Arrange the meat and the potatoes on a serving dish, drizzle with the cooking juices and serve hot.

Sardines a beccafico

16 sardines, 100 g breadcrumbs, 2 tablespoons grated
pecorino cheese, 4 salted anchovies, 1 small onion,
1 stick of celery, 2 garlic cloves, 2 bunches parsley,
2 teaspoons capers, 8 green olives, all-purpose flour,
1 kg tomato pulp, ½ glass dry white wine,
extra-virgin olive oil, ½ glass vinegar, salt.

Clean and bone the sardines, splitting them open. Wash them with water and vinegar (50/50) and leave them to dry on a clean cloth. Prepare the stuffing: mix together the breadcrumbs and the grated pecorino cheese, crush one clove of garlic, one bunch of parsley, a coffee spoon of crushed capers, two finely chopped anchovy fillets, a pinch of salt, a sprinkle of white wine and four tablespoons of olive oil. Mix well all the ingredients and spread the mixture over eight sardines. Cover with the remaining eight sardines, roll them up and tie with some butcher's twine. Cover the sardine rolls in flour and fry in a pan containing a little olive oil. Drain and leave to dry on paper towels. Chop the onion and garlic, slice the celery and sauté in oil in a big saucepan. Add the capers, the olives (pitted and crushed), the anchovies and a bunch of crushed parsley. Pour over the tomato pulp (if it is too dense, you can dilute in by adding a glass of water), season with salt and bring to the boil. Lower the heat and leave to cook for about fifteen minutes over medium heat. Add the sardine rolls and stir over very low heat for a further ten minutes. Remove from the heat and drain the sardine rolls with a skimmer. Remove the butcher's twine and serve hot, accompanied with their sauce.

"Beccafico" ia a little bird that in Sicily become very fat eating the "fico" fruits, that are figs. They are as fat as these stuffed sardines.

Sicilian cannoli

For cannoli shells: 200 g extra-fine flour, 1 tablespoon icing sugar, 20 g butter, 1 egg, 1 teaspoon unsweetened cocoa powder, salt, ½ glass dry white wine.

For the filling: 800 g fresh ricotta cheese, 160 g sugar, 50 g minced candied cedar peel (or candied pumpkin), 2 tablespoons unsweetened cocoa powder, 40 g dark chocolate. Garnish: 8 candied cherries, minced candied orange peel, 2 tablespoons icing sugar. Special equipment: a capacious high-sided frying pan, 1 l peanut oil, 10 metal cylinders (for rolling the pastry round: they can be found in shops selling specialised kitchen utensils).

Prepare the *cannoli* shells: mix evenly the flour, the icing sugar, the cocoa and a pinch of salt. Make a well in the middle and add the softened butter and the beaten egg yolk (keep the egg white aside). Knead thoroughly, adding the white wine until you have a smooth, consistent dough. Wrap the dough in a cotton cloth and leave for about half an hour in a cool, dark place. Unwrap the dough and flatten it with a rolling-pin: the pastry must be about 3 mm thick (if you use a pasta-machine, set it on n°3). Cut out circles (about 10 cm in diameter) and roll them around the oiled metal cylinders, pressing down where the edges meet and using some egg white to seal them. Heat the oil in the high-sided frying pan and fry the *cannoli* shells a few at a time, turning them with metal tongs until they are evenly golden all over (a couple of minutes should be enough). Drain and leave to cool and dry on absorbent paper. Once you have removed the metal cylinders, the shells are ready to be filled. If you are not using them straight away, you can store them in a box (carefully closed). Now prepare the filling: in a bowl, beat together the ricotta cheese with the sugar until you have a very smooth, creamy mixture, then stir in the minced candied cedar peel. If the cream is too soft, you can add some sponge cake crumbles and 50 g of roughly-grated white chocolate. Fill the *cannoli* shells with this mixture. If you want, you can fill the *cannoli* shells only halfway with the ricotta cheese mixture and then add two tablespoons of unsweetened cocoa powder and some roughly-grated dark chocolate to the rest of the cream, using it to complete the filling of your *cannoli* shells. Dust the *cannoli* with the icing sugar using a strainer. Garnish the white cream end with candied orange peel and the chocolate cream end with half of a candied cherry. *Cannoli* should be served straight away, in order to enjoy their crispy shell and the creamy filling.

"Cannolo" means "little tube".
Is a sicilian pastry dessert.

1 'pan di Spagna' sponge cake, about 20 cm in diameter. 400 g of fresh ricotta, 100g of sugar, 100 g of bittersweet chocolate, 250 g of mixed candied fruits (citron, cherries, orange peel), 250 g of caster sugar – (or a pat of pistachio almond paste of about 300 g), orange liqueur (or, if you prefer, the juice of two oranges)

Cassata Siciliana

Cut the pan di Spagna sponge into three disks each about a centimetre thick. Place the disks on the bottom of a cake pan. Cut the second disk cut into strips and use these to line the sides of the cake tin. Crumble the pieces of plan di Spagna that are left over and put to one side. Mix the ricotta with the sugar and two tablespoons of orange liqueur, working them with a fork and spoon to dissolve the sugar and obtain a smooth velvety mix. Add the pan di Spagna crumbs, the broken chocolate and 100 g of crumbled mixed candied fruit and mix together well. Wet the bottom and the edges of the pan di Spagna (that line the edge of the cake pan) with a little orange liqueur diluted 50-50 with water and pour into the mix the ricotta, spreading it out evenly. Cover this with the third circle of pan di Spagna, which should also be moistened through. Leave all to cool in the fridge for a couple of houses and then take out of the fridge, turning the cake-tin over carefully and placing it on a tray. Dissolve the sugar in a frying pan with three tablespoons' of water and use the blade of a knife to spread it evenly over the surface and the borders of the dessert. According to the original recipe there was, instead of the glaze on the top, a covering of a thin layer of pistachio almond paste (sometimes just around the edges). Decorate the cassata as you wish with the remaining candied fruits, some whole and some sliced. Put back in the fridge for a few hours until the whole is fully set.

250 g extra-fine flour, 100 g sugar, 50 g almonds,
½ bag baking powder, 1 tea spoon ground clove,
ground cinnamon.
Butter and flour for the baking-tray.

Mostaccioli

These are cakes in the traditional southern Italy cuisine.
The name comes from the Latin "mustaceum" because some similar cakes were made in the past with knust.

Zucchero

Toast the almonds in the oven (without peeling them), then ground them finely. Sieve the flour and the baking powder and shape it into a well. Add the ground clove, a pinch of cinnamon powder, the almonds and the sugar. Mix well all the ingredients, gradually adding warm water until you have a soft, smooth dough. Using a rolling pin, roll out the dough to a sheet 0,5 cm thick and cut out different shapes using cookie cutters. Lay the cookies on the baking-tray (previously greased and sprinkled with flour) and decorate their surface tracing lines with the side of a fork (or make simple drawings using icing sugar whisked together with egg whites).
Bake the *mostaccioli* in a pre-heated oven at 190 °C for about 20 minutes. Leave to cool and serve, or store in a box.

Carasau bread
("music sheet" bread)
with cheese and honey

4 sheets of Carasau bread,
400 g soft cheese from Sardinia
(casizolu, fresh caciocavallo, caciotta,
sweet Sardinian cheese or fresh pecorino cheese),
50 g honey.

Break into large pieces the *Carasau* bread and arrange in a baking tray.
Cut the cheese into thin slices and lay it on top of the bread. Bake at
200 °C, until the cheese melts. Remove from the oven
and pour a little honey over each toast. Leave to melt and serve.

*This bread is called Carasau but also "music sheet"
bread because if you break it, it "sounds".
It's thin and crispy, usually in the form of a dish,
half meter wide. This kind of bread, if it is kept dry,
can last up to a year.
It was conceived, who used to stay away for months.*

Spaghetti with bottarga

400 g spaghetti, 30-50 g bottarga
(mullet eggs preserved in salt),
1 clove garlic, extra-virgin olive oil,
1 sprig of parsley, salt.

Buy fresh bottarga and grate the quantity you need. Meanwhile,
heat abundant salted water to cook the spaghetti.
While the spaghetti is cooking, heat some olive oil in a large saucepan.
Add some chopped garlic and parsley, then add a third
of the grated bottarga.
Drain the pasta when al dente and transfer to the pan with the olive oil,
together with a couple of tablespoons of cooking water
previously put aside.
Stir well, leave to fry for a couple of minutes
and then add the rest of the bottarga. Serve hot.

Malloreddus "alla campidanese"

(Sardinian dumplings with sausage, tomato and saffron)

360 g gnocchetti sardi (small dumplings, typical from Sardinia), 200 g fresh sausage, 1 red onion, 1 kg ripe tomatoes, 100 g grated Sardinian pecorino cheese, 1 small bunch of basil, 4 tablespoons extra-virgin olive oil, 1 sachet of saffron, salt. The diminutive of malloru (bull in Sardinian dialect), malloreddus means 'fat little calves'.

Blanch the tomatoes in hot water for about 3 minutes, then rinse with cold running water, peel them, remove the seeds and chop finely, then pass the tomatoes through a food mill. Sauté the onion finely chopped in a large saucepan with olive oil, add the chopped sausage, previously skinned, and leave to brown for five minutes. Add the tomato pulp, partially cover the saucepan and leave to cook for about half an hour over medium heat, stirring from time to time. Season with salt, add the chopped basil and the saffron. Leave to simmer for five more minutes, in order to reduce and thicken the sauce. Cook the dumplings in plenty of salted water, drain as soon as they rise to the surface and dress with the sauce, sprinkling with a lot of grated pecorino cheese.

"alla campidanese" means Campidano style. Campidano is a plain located in the south-western area of Sardinia.

1 suckling pig, aromatic herbs (sprigs of myrtle and rosemary, thyme), salt.

Porcheddu carriaxiu

This recipe is a symbol of Sardinian culture: more than a meal, to roast a suckling pig is an event. The pig is roasted in an earth oven outdoor, and the whole process is quite complex. Since it takes a long time to get the pig ready, make sure you start preparing a few hours before lunchtime.

Dig a large hole in the ground, then layer it with many large stones. Build a bonfire over the stones to get them hot all the way through. When the logs have turned into embers, take out quickly some of the stones and place the aromatic herbs in the pit. Lower the piglet in the pit, wrap it in herbs in order to isolate it from the embers and then cover it with the hot stones you removed. After that, refill the hole with earth, embers, coal and hot stones to keep the heat in. Leave to cook for 3-4 hours, then take the piglet out from the hole and serve hot, sprinkled with salt.

"Porceddu" in sardinian dialect is the suckling pig.

2 medium size lobsters, 2 Tropea onions (red onions), 400 g cherry tomatoes, 2 bay leaves, 1 lemon, extra-virgin olive oil, 1 glass vinegar, oregano, salt, pepper.

Catalan-style lobster

Wash and halve the cherry tomatoes. Peel the onions, cut off the root end and slice the onions in whole round slices. Separate the rings and boil for a few minutes in hot water, adding a glass of vinegar and a pinch of salt. Drain and leave to cool.

Fill a large stockpot with water, a pinch of salt and two bay leaves and bring to a boil. When the water has come to a rolling boil, plunge the lobsters headfirst into the pot. Cook the lobsters for about fifteen minutes, then lift them out of the water with tongs and let them cool on a cutting board. Use kitchen shears (kitchen scissors) to cut both sides of the shell under the lobster's belly, in order to split the lobster into two halves. Clean out the entrails and gills, then lay the lobsters on a grill and roast for ten minutes. When ready, arrange the halves in dishes over a layer of cherry tomatoes and onion rings, previously dressed with olive oil, salt and oregano. Drizzle with lemon juice, season with salt and pepper and serve.

Sardinian-style sea bream

2 sea breams, 1 onion, 1 garlic clove,
2 courgettes, 2 ripe tomatoes, 50 g grated pecorino cheese,
2 tablespoons all-purpose flour,
½ teaspoon oregano,
2 tablespoons extra-virgin olive oil,
2 tablespoons aromatic vinegar, salt.

Wash the sea breams inside and out with cold, fresh water. Remove the bones and the skin, then boil for 5 minutes in a little water with some vinegar and a pinch of salt. Drain the breams and remove all the fish bones, then cover the fish in flour and put aside. Keep the cooking water.

Chop the onion finely, crush the garlic clove and slice the courgettes, sauté in a large frying pan and after a couple of minutes add the sea breams. Add the tomatoes (previously skinned and chopped), pour some cooking water, add some oregano and a pinch of salt. Cover the pan with a lid and cook over low heat for about 10 minutes. Sprinkle with pecorino cheese, leave to melt, then remove from the heat and serve immediately.

Casadinas
(or formagelle, cheese tarts)

For the pastry: 750 g extra-fine flour, 50 lard, salt.
For the filling: 500 fresh cheese (ricotta cheese or similar),
100 g sugar, 2 eggs, the grated peel of 1 lemon,
100 g raisins, extra-fine flour.

Leave the raisins to soak in lukewarm water for a few hours. Prepare the pastry: mix the flour, the lard, a pinch of salt and a little warm water, adding it a little at a time. Knead thoroughly until you have a firm, smooth dough. Cover it with a cloth and leave to rest in a cold place for a few hours.

Meanwhile, push the ricotta through a fine sieve into a mixing bowl, add the sugar, the eggs, the raisins (previously drained), the lemon zest and a couple of tablespoons of flour.

Flatten the dough with a rolling pin until you get a thin sheet. Cut out discs with a glass or a round cutter (diameter: about 10 cm), then place a heaped teaspoon of filling in the center of each disc, gently pressing it down to flatten a little. Fold the sides of the disc up, pinching them to form a cup around the filling. Arrange the *casadinas* - in Gallura also called *formagelle* - on a baking paper lined baking tray, then place the tray in a pre-heated oven (150 °C) for about 40 minutes. Once the filling is well browned, remove from the oven and brush with honey. Serve the ricotta cheese *casadinas* warm or cold - whereas fresh cheese *casadinas* are to be served cold.

Amaretti biscuits

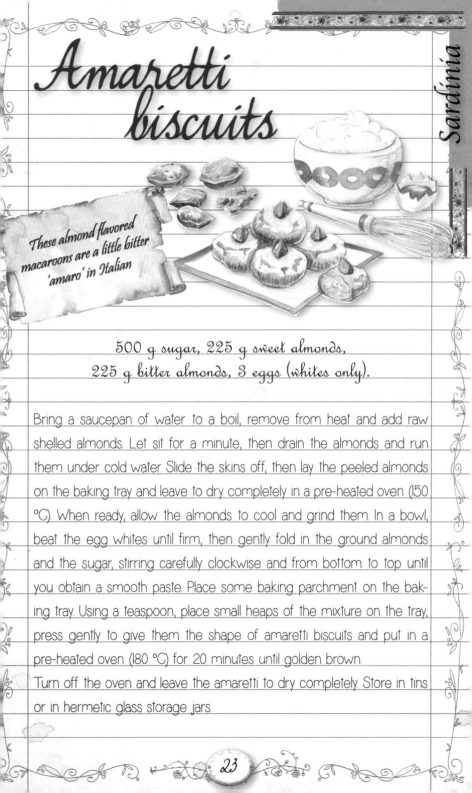

These almond flavored macaroons are a little bitter 'amaro' in Italian

500 g sugar, 225 g sweet almonds,
225 g bitter almonds, 3 eggs (whites only).

Bring a saucepan of water to a boil, remove from heat and add raw shelled almonds. Let sit for a minute, then drain the almonds and run them under cold water. Slide the skins off, then lay the peeled almonds on the baking tray and leave to dry completely in a pre-heated oven (150 °C). When ready, allow the almonds to cool and grind them. In a bowl, beat the egg whites until firm, then gently fold in the ground almonds and the sugar, stirring carefully clockwise and from bottom to top until you obtain a smooth paste. Place some baking parchment on the baking tray. Using a teaspoon, place small heaps of the mixture on the tray, press gently to give them the shape of amaretti biscuits and put in a pre-heated oven (180 °C) for 20 minutes until golden brown.

Turn off the oven and leave the amaretti to dry completely. Store in tins or in hermetic glass storage jars.

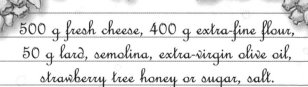

500 g fresh cheese, 400 g extra-fine flour,
50 g lard, semolina, extra-virgin olive oil,
strawberry tree honey or sugar, salt.

SEBADA
(Sardinian cheese pastry)

Prepare the mixture by sifting the flour into the shape of a well, then add the lard, warm water and a teaspoon of salt. Knead until you have a smooth, consistent dough, then cover the dough with a cloth and let it sit in a cool place. Chop the cheese in small cubes, melt it in a non-stick pan with 2,5 dl of water over a low flame and add some semolina, until you have a dense cream. Leave to cool, and then form little balls. Flatten them with your hands and put them aside on a clean cloth. Roll out the pastry mixture on a sheet and cut out circular bases with a diameter of 10 cm. Arrange the cheese filling on a base and top it with another disc of pastry, pressing well the edges together. Continue until you've used up all the cheese and the pastry. Once they are ready, fry them in plenty of olive oil and serve hot, covered in strawberry tree honey or sugar.

Pappa col pomodoro
(bread and tomato soup)

500 g ripe tomatoes, 2 cloves garlic, ½ red hot pepper,
fresh basil, 300 g stale bread, 1 l vegetable broth,
4 tablespoons extra-virgin olive oil, salt, pepper.

Sauté the crushed garlic in some olive oil. Chop the tomatoes and the pepper and add them to the garlic. Add the crushed basil leaves and leave to cook for about ten minutes.

Cut the bread into large cubes and stir well, until the bread is well mixed with the tomato sauce. When the sauce starts to dry up, add hot broth and season with salt and pepper. Cover and leave to cook over low heat for about 15 minutes, until it becomes a *"pappa"*, a mush. Add some more broth if the soup becomes too thick.

Turn off the fire and leave to sit for an hour. Stir well, drizzle with olive oil, garnish with basil leaves and serve lukewarm.

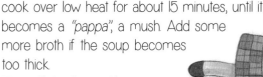

Fried onion rings

2 Tropea onions (red onions),
150 g extra-fine flour, extra-virgin olive oil,
1 glass apple cider vinegar,
ground hot chilli, salt.

In a medium bowl combine the flour, a tablespoon of olive oil, a pinch of salt and a pinch of hot chilli. Pour some cold water while stirring with a whisk, in order to get a dense, fluid and smooth batter. Leave to sit in the fridge for half an hour. Meanwhile, peel the onions and slice them, then separate the rings and leave in a bowl with water and vinegar for about ten minutes. Drain the onion rings and dip them in the batter (previously carefully stirred). Fry in plenty of hot olive oil until golden brown. Drain with a skimmer and place on kitchen paper to dry. Leave to cool for a few minutes and serve.

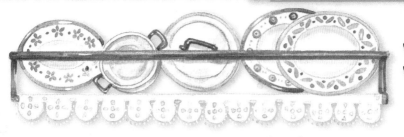

Lamb ribs alla calabrese

*800 g of lambs' ribs, 500 g of ripe tomatoes, 1 onion,
1 green bell pepper, 1 yellow bell pepper, 100 g of green olives,
1 sprig of parsley, 8 tablespoonsful of extra-virgin olive oil,
salt and pepper*

Heat four tablespoonsful of olive oil in a frying pan and slowly brown the thinly sliced onion together with the diced peppers (having tailed them and removed the seeds and white ribbing inside). Add the peeled, seeded and thinly sliced tomatoes, the pitted and halved olives, salt and pepper. Continue cooking over a low heat on the now covered pan for another 10 to 15 minutes. With the remaining olive oil slowly and evenly fry the ribs in a pan, turning them through each side. When they appear well cooked, drain them and put them in the pan with the vegetables, add the chopped parsley, mix well and leave to rest and for the flavours to mingle for another 5 minutes.
Then bring the dish straight to the table, serving with home-made bread.

Rabbit *"alla cacciatora"*
(hunter style)

1 rabbit, 150 g bacon (in thin slices), 4 cloves garlic,
1 sprig rosemary, 1 teaspoon fennel seeds,
4 tablespoons extra-virgin olive oil,
½ teaspoon ground hot chilli, salt.

Wash the rabbit (already cleaned) with cold running water and pat dry with a cloth.

Chop the bacon, crush two cloves of garlic and some rosemary leaves, mix together with half a teaspoon of fennel seeds and stuff the rabbit with this mixture. Baste with olive oil the rabbit, rub it with crushed garlic, sprinkle with ground red hot chili pepper and fennel seeds. Wrap the rabbit up in bacon slices, then wrap it all in aluminum foil and place in an oven-safe casserole. Cook in a pre-heated oven (180 °C) for an hour. When ready, unwrap the rabbit and cut it up. Serve hot, with its cooking juices.

400 g minced pork, 100 g 'nduja (or other soft spicy salami),
2 eggs, 1 Tropea onion (red onion), 1 clove garlic,
1 sprig parsley, 2 tablespoons grated Parmesan,
50 g stale bread, 1 lemon, extra-virgin olive oil, salt,
ground black pepper.

Soften the bread by soaking it in water, then remove and gently squeeze out excess water. Chop up the salami, the onion and the garlic, mix them with the minced meat, the eggs, the grated Parmesan, the bread, a pinch of pepper and a pinch of salt. When you have obtained a smooth mixture, divide into parts and form medallions of about 8 cm diameter and ½ cm thick. Cook on the griddle until golden, a few minutes per side. Season with oil and lemon juice, then serve with vegetables. Alternatively, simmer a chopped onion in a pan, season with salt, oregano and a drizzle of vinegar and cook the medallions until golden.

Pork medallions with 'nduja

(spicy spreadable meat from Calabria)

Swordfish "a ghiotta"

"A ghiotta" means a special and traditional way to prepare the swordfish.

4 slices swordfish, 1 onion,
2 cloves garlic, 1 carrot,
 1 stick of celery (with its leaves),
2 sprigs parsley, ½ half a hot chilli,
100 g black olives,
1 tablespoons capers,
500 g ripe tomatoes, 2 tablespoons all-purpose flour,
4 tablespoons extra-virgin olive oil, salt, pepper.

Dust the fish with flour and fry in olive oil for a few minutes, then leave to dry on kitchen paper. Chop the vegetables and simmer in the pan, add the capers, the crumbled half a hot chilli, the olives (previously pitted and cut in two)
Simmer for about ten minutes in a covered pan, and then add the fish, the crushed parsley and half a glass of water. Season with salt and pepper and continue cooking for about 10-15 minutes over a low heat.

1,5 mussels, 2 cloves garlic,
2 sprigs parsley, 120 g breadcrumbs,
3 tablespoons grated Parmesan,
4 tablespoons extra-virgin olive oil.

Mussels au gratin

Scrub, clean and wash the mussels under running water. Cut off the beards and if any mussels are opened, discard them.

Put the mussels in a large saucepan (without any water), cover with a lid and leave over high heat until they open (about 5 minutes) and transfer the mussels to a bowl with a slotted spoon. Discard any unopened shells and the top half of all the mussels. Filter the liquid released by the mussel, put aside in a cup and drizzle with olive oil. In a bowl mix the breadcrumbs, the grated Parmesan, the crushed garlic and the parsley finely chopped. Arrange the mussels in a baking tray and sprinkle the mixture over the mussels. Drizzle with the cooking juices previously put aside and bake in a pre-heated oven (180 °C) until the breadcrumbs are light brown (about 15 minutes). Serve immediately.

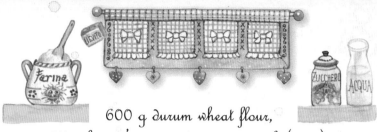

600 g durum wheat flour,
25 g brewer's yeast, 1 teaspoon salt (12 g).

Homemade bread

Prepare the *"lievitino"* (diminutive of *"lievito"*, yeast): dissolve the yeast in a little lukewarm water, add a little flour to make it a sponge (but still quite liquid), cover with a cloth and leave the mixture to prove for an hour, until it rises and starts showing little bubbles on its surface.

Form a well with the flour on a work surface, pour the *"lievitino"* and start kneading thoroughly, adding enough water to obtain a smooth dough. Add a little salt, previously dissolved in water, and keep kneading, until the dough is smooth and stretchy. Form a ball of the dough, dust with flour and cover with a cloth, leaving to prove for two hours. Once the dough has doubled in size, knead again and divide into two loaves, giving them a round or an oval shape. With a sharp knife, make deep cuts (a cross, or a diamond pattern) across the top of the loaf. Lay the loaves on baking paper dusted with flour, place on a baking tray and leave to prove for 30 minutes. Pre-heat the oven (220 °C), bake the bread for 15 minutes, then lower the temperature to 200 °C and leave to bake for a further 40 minutes. The loaf is cooked when it's risen and golden brown; it must sound hollow when tapped on the bottom. Turn off the oven, open the door and leave the bread to dry in the oven for 5 minutes, then wrap the loaf in a cloth and leave to cool.

500 g extra-fine flour,
1 teaspoon fennel seeds or aniseed,
1 glass dry white wine,
5 tablespoons extra-virgin olive oil, salt.

Tarallini

(diminutive of 'taralli',
savory Italian snack food,
similar to bagels.)

Mix the flour with the olive oil, a coffee spoon of salt and the fennel seeds (or the aniseed). Start kneading thoroughly and slowly incorporate the white wine until you have a consistent, soft dough. Keep kneading for about 10 minutes, until the dough is smooth and consistent. Leave to sit for 30 minutes. Divide and shape the dough into small ropes of about 10 cm in length and form rings by pinching the ends together.

In a pot, boil some salted water and drop in the *tarallini*, about ten at a time. As soon as they float to the top, remove them from the water with a slotted spoon and leave them to dry on a cloth. Once all the *tarallini* are ready, arrange them on a greased oven tray and cook in a hot oven (180 °C) for about 30 minutes, until they are golden brown and crisp. Leave to cool and serve cold.

Orecchiette *alla barese*

400 g orecchiette ('little ears' in Italian),
8 thin slices veal (or horse meat), 8 thin slices lard,
500 g tomato pulp, 1 onion, 1 clove garlic, 1 sprig parsley,
150 g cacio cheese from Apulia (or pecorino cheese),
50 g breadcrumbs, 1 glass red wine,
4 tablespoons extra-virgin olive oil, salt.

According to some of the oldest recipes, you can use horse meat instead of veal. Lay on top of each meat slice a slice of lard, sprinkle with breadcrumbs, minced parsley leaves, two thin slices of cacio cheese (a kind of hard ricotta cheese, also called 'cacio ricotta'). Roll up tightly and secure with a toothpick. Crush the garlic, slice the onion and sauté in a pan with olive oil. When they are golden brown, remove the garlic and place the meat rolls in the pan. Leave to brown for about 5 minutes, then pour the wine and simmer until it evaporates. Add the tomato pulp, season with salt and simmer for about 20 minutes over a low heat, stirring from time to time. Bring to the boil a saucepan of salted water, then add the *orecchiette* and drain when al dente. Dress the pasta with the sauce, add a couple of meat rolls to each plate, sprinkle with grated cacio cheese and serve.

Orecchiette with **broccoli rabe**

320 g orecchiette, 600 g broccoli rabe, 4 anchovies in oil
2 cloves garlic, 4 tablespoons extra-virgin olive oil, salt.

Wash the broccoli rabe carefully, then trim leaving only a little bit of stem. Use only tender leaves and broccoli tops. Cook for about 5 minutes in hot salted water, then add the orecchiette to the pan and cook until al dente. Meanwhile, heat some olive oil and add the chopped garlic in a saucepan. After a couple of minutes add the anchovies and blend them into the oil. Remove the cloves of garlic and leave the sauce to simmer over low heat. Drain the pasta and the broccoli rabe, transfer to the saucepan and stir into the sauce for a couple of minutes. Serve immediately.

"Orecchiette", that mean "small ears", are a kind of home-made pasta typical of Puglia.
"Alla barese" means "Bari style". Bari is the most important city of Puglia.

250 g slices white bread (crust removed),
250 g low moisture packaged mozzarella
for pizza-making), 150 g sliced cooked ham,
1 glass milk, 2 eggs,
100 g breadcrumbs, peanut oil, salt.

Divide each slice of bread in order to obtain 20 rectangles. Pour the milk into a soup bowl, add the eggs, season with salt and beat the mixture with a fork. Prepare 10 slices of mozzarella and 10 slices of ham; they should be both slightly smaller than the bread slices, in order to leave a little margin around the edges unfilled with cheese when you prepare the sandwiches. Warm the oil in a frying pan over medium heat.

Quickly dip ten bread slices into the egg mixture, drain and arrange on a tray. Place the mozzarella and the ham over the bread slices and top with the rest of the bread, previously dipped into the egg mixture. You now have ten little sandwiches: press the edges together with your fingers to help seal and dredge in the bread crumbs. Fry, turning once, until the sandwiches are crisp and the cheese has melted. Drain, leave to dry on absorbent kitchen paper and serve while still hot.

"In carrozza" means "on a carriage" as the mozzarella is driven on the slices of bread.

Mozzarelle in carrozza
(fried mozzarella sandwiches)

CAFFÈ

The coffee bean is the seed from some trees that are typically found in some tropical areas and belong to the large Rubiaceae family of plants. Of the many species identified the most widespread are the Arabica and the Robusta. Coffee is though usually drunk as a blend, mixing the different beans from several coffee varieties. The obtainable blends are infinite and can be customised to taste.

According to the saying, coffee requires the three S's of seated, sizzling and scrounged, but if you want to make yourself it is best as follows:

fill the coffee pot to just below the steam valve with spring water or at least water that is not to hard;

pour the coffee powder, best if just ground, into the filter without tamping it down;

place the coffee pot over a gentle flame,

switch off the flame as soon as the coffee pot begins to make its percolating sound;

turn the coffee before pouring it into the cup in order to mix the dense lower part with that more watery top;

ideally pour the coffee into heated small porcelain cups.

Just pause for a few minutes in the morning at a well-organised coffee bar to see all the many different ways the Italians like to drink their coffee:

- caffè espresso, which may be served in normal or in glass cups;
- caffè ristretto, just a few drops of the drink at a time, but with an intense aroma and very low caffeine content;
- caffè corretto, with grappa or other regional spirit added:
- cappuccino, or coffee with foaming milk, which is known as a marocchino if decorated with chocolate powder;
- caffè macchiato, with hot or cold cream added to taste;
- caffè decaffeinato, or decaffeinated, in which case the blend has been industrially washed to remove the caffeine from the beans;
- caffè lungo, obtained by allowing more water than usual to flow into the coffee, which becomes caffè Americano if there is a lot of water, which may be up to 80 cc per cup;
this contains more caffeine than is normal.
- caffè d'orzo, which bears the name coffee out of convention though it is not made from the coffee bean but from toasted barley.

- macchiatone, which has become de rigeuer in recent times and is served in a large cup, half way between caffè macchiato and cappuccino;
- caffè shakerato, which is usually drunk in the summer, is made by shaking the coffee in a shaker, with or without sugar and ice... with many other versions available depending on the place and the fashion of the time.

CAFFE' ALLA VALDOSTANA is made in the typical "coppa dell'amicizia" or friendship bowl which has many spouts or lips so all those seated can drink from the same vessel, passing it from one to the other.
4 small coffee cups of coffee, 3 glasses of grappa, 3 glasses of Genepi liqueur, 10 cloves, 1 cinnamon stick, 1 lemon, 1 orange and 4 teaspoons of sugar.

Pour the boiling hot coffee into the vessel, along with the liqueurs, the spices and the lemon peel all sweetened with the sugar. Flambé with a long naked flame and then, when the alcohol has burned off, put the lid on the vessel and enjoy the drink in company.

LA MORETTA DI FANO is a drink for a seafaring population for whom a coffee with liqueur warmed them up for a hard day's fishing. Into the typical inn glass goes a spoons of sugar and a little lemon peel, then a dose of 'moretta' to taste, i.e. a liqueur made up of a blend of rum, brandy and anise. The whole blend is heated by steam to dissolve the sugar and partly burn off the alcohol. At the end the caffè espresso is added.

IL BICERIN PIEMONTESE is a non-alcoholic drink in which there are layers of coffee, melted chocolate and milk cream. The drink may also be served with whipped cream or the addition of Gianduia liqueur.

To make CAFFE' ALLA NAPOLETANA you need to have the right equipment, that is to say the Neapolitan moka. You fill it like a normal moka but it is placed on a lively flame and as soon as the steam valve issues forth steam it must be taken of the flame and turned upside down. Get the "coppetiello" ready, which is a sheet of kitchen roll shaped into a cone that is inserted into the lip of the coffee pot as soon as it is turned upright, in order to hold in the aroma of coffee and stop it escaping.

Caprese salad

3 buffalo mozzarellas, 4 medium-sized salad
tomatoes, a few fresh basil leaves,
extra virgin olive oil, salt and pepper.

Caprese is the simplest and best known of the salad recipes from
the Campania region, and is ideal for the summertime. Like with all
simple dishes its tastiness depends on the ingredients being top quality.
Thoroughly and carefully wash the tomatoes and slice them thinly, removing
most of the seeds and place them on a sloping surface after lightly salting
them. This will allow some of the juices to drain away. In the meantime
cut the mozzarellas into slices and place these too on a sloping surface for
the water to run away. Finally place the tomato and mozzarella in alternate
layers in a pleasing arrangement. Drizzle with a little olive oil and serve fresh,
garnished with some small basil leaves.

Pizza Margherita

500 g flour, 25 g fresh yeast, 1 coffee spoon
sugar, 400 g mozzarella cheese,
4 peeled tomatoes cut into thin slices,
a few leaves of basil,
extra-virgin olive oil, salt.

Form a well with the flour. Dissolve the sugar and the crumbled yeast in a spoonful of lukewarm water, then pour the mixture in the centre of the well. Add the salt (dissolved in a little water), a couple of tablespoons of olive oil and sufficient water to knead. Knead thoroughly adding some water if necessary, until the dough becomes soft and elastic. Form a ball with the dough, dust with flour, place in a bowl and cover with a cloth. Leave to rise in a warm place for about one and a half hours.

Once the dough has risen and doubled its size, divide it into four portions and roll out on a floured surface to a round or rectangular sheet - thin if you like you pizza to be crusty, thicker if you like it to be soft. Pre-heat the oven (220 °C). Cover the pizzas with the peeled tomatoes, spreading the pulp and the juice with a spoon. Sprinkle with salt, drizzle with olive oil and bake for about 10-15 minutes, until the edges are golden brown. Remove from the oven and add the mozzarella cheese, previously cut into small cubes. Put the pizza back into the oven for 5 minutes, or until the cheese has melted. Remove from the oven, decorate with chopped basil leaves and serve immediately.

400 g spaghetti (also called linguine or trenette), 300 g baby octopus or squids, 500 g clams, 500 g mussels, 400 g ripe and firm tomatoes, 2 cloves garlic, 2 sprigs parsley, 1 glass dry white wine, 4 tablespoons extra-virgin olive oil, ground pepper (or red hot ground pepper).

(traditional kind of pasta named spaghetti with seafood)

Spaghetti alla marinara

Scrub and de-beard the shells of the mussels and clams, then wash under running water. Rinse and clean the squids. Put the shellfish in a large saucepan with one crushed garlic clove, some parsley leaves and half a glass of wine. Heat over high heat the covered saucepan for about 10 minutes, until all the shells open. Turn off the heat, strain the cooking juices and put them aside. Put aside half a dozen clams and mussels and split the shells in two, discarding the empty half. Peel the tomatoes by blanching them in hot water, then remove the seeds and chop finely. In a frying pan, pour 4 tablespoons of olive oil, one crushed garlic clove and the crushed parsley. Sauté for a couple of minutes, add the squids, pour the white wine and leave to cook for about 15 minutes. Add the clams, the mussels, the tomato pulp and some of the seafood cooking juices. You won't need to add any salt since the cooking juices are really tasty. If you want, you can sprinkle the sauce with some freshly ground black or red pepper. Leave to cook for another 15-20 minutes over medium heat, allowing the sauce to reduce. Boil the *spaghetti* in plenty of salted hot water, drain when al dente and mix in the sauce. Garnish with the mussels and clams in the half shell and serve immediately.

Spaghetti

360 spaghetti, 1,5 kg clams,
2 cloves garlic, 1 sprig parsley, 1 ripe and firm tomato,
½ glass dry white wine,
4 tablespoons extra-virgin olive oil, ½ red hot pepper.

Clean the shellfish under cold running water and leave to purge in plenty of salted water for at least one hour to get rid of any sand. Drain and put in a saucepan (without any water) over high heat, cover the pan and let the clams open (about 5 minutes), then drain the shellfish, strain the cooking juices and put them aside. Discard any unopened or broken clam, separate the mollusks from the shells and keep aside a dozen to garnish the plates.

In a saucepan, sauté the crushed garlic, add the wine, the chopped parsley, the crushed red hot pepper, the tomato previously peeled and chopped. Cover the saucepan and cook for 5 minutes, then add the clams and half a glass of their cooking juices (you probably won't need to add any salt, because this sauce is quite tasty). Bring back to the boil and cook for a further 5 minutes.

In the meantime, bring a pot of salted water to the boil, add the spaghetti, cook and drain when al dente. Mix with the sauce, garnish with the clams previously put aside and serve immediately.

with clams

Rum Babà

For the babà dough:
240 g extra-fine flour, 20 g fresh yeast,
4 eggs, 80 g butter, 30 g sugar, 1 pinch of salt.
For the coating: 200 g sugar,
1 organic lemon zest, 2 small glasses rum.
Butter for the babà moulds.

Dissolve the yeast in a little lukewarm water, add 50 g of flour and mix thoroughly. Put the dough aside, in order to let it rise. When it has doubled its size, put it in a large bowl, add the eggs and previously softened butter and cut into pieces. Cream the mixture, gradually add the flour, sugar and salt. Keep kneading the dough until you have a soft, elastic dough which doesn't stick to the sides of the bowl when lifted. The dough should also show 'bubbles' on its surface. Cover the bowl with a cloth and leave to rise for about one hour. In the meantime, butter the *babà* moulds. When the dough has doubled its size, fill the moulds half way through and leave to rise until the dough reaches the top of the mould. Bake in a pre-heated oven (180 °C) for about 15-20 minutes, until the *babàs* are golden brown. In the meantime, prepare the coating: melt the sugar over the heat, with 250 ml water and the lemon zest. Take it off the heat, add the rum and leave to cool. Slowly dip the warm *babàs* in plenty of syrup, allowing it all to soak in thoroughly. Gently squeeze out excess syrup and lay the *babàs* on a tray. Cover with a cloth and sprinkle with rum before serving. If you want, you can prepare a delicious coating with apricot jam, by heating some apricot jam with a little water and spreading it over the *babàs*. If you do not wish to use alcohol - or if you are preparing *babàs* for children - you can substitute rum for lemon or rum flavor.

For the pastry: 500 g extra-fine flour, 200 g butter, 200 g sugar, 3 whole eggs and 1 yolk, 1 lemon zest, 1 sachet baking powder.

For the filling: 600 g ricotta cheese, 500 g sugar, ½ l milk, 500 pre-cooked wheat, 8 eggs, 40 g butter, 70 candied lime, ½ coffee spoon ground cinnamon, 1 vanilla bean (or 1 sachet vanilla extract), 1 teaspoon orange flower water, 1 lemon zest, salt. Butter and flour for the cake-tin.

Pastiera napoletana
(Neapolitan Easter grain pie)

Prepare the shortcrust pastry mixing all the ingredients, handling the dough as little as possible and working rapidly. Butter the cake-tin and sprinkle it with flour, then roll out about two thirds of the pastry about half a centimetre thick and line the cake-tin. Cut out the remaining pastry into strips about two centimetres wide, arrange on a dish (you will use it to form a grid pattern over the cake) and put the cake-tin and the dish with the pastry stripes in the fridge until needed. If you prefer, you can buy a packet of fresh short crust pastry. In a saucepan cook the wheat with the milk, the butter, a pinch of salt and the lemon zest. Leave over moderate heat for about 15-20 minutes, stirring carefully until you have a creamy mixture. Remove from heat and leave to cool. Blend the ricotta cheese and the sugar together and pass the cream through a sieve into a large bowl, add two whole eggs and five egg yolks, reserving the egg whites for later. Add the wheat mixture, the cinnamon, the candied lime, the vanilla extract and the orange flower water. Beat the five egg whites until stiff and fold them in carefully to the mixture, stirring from bottom to top. Pre-heat the oven (170°-180 °C) and pour the creamy mixture in the cake-tin (in Naples, this special cake-tin is called *'il ruoto'*, 'round-shaped), a round aluminum tin, 4-5 cm deep, with smooth edges. Decorate the surface with the pastry strips previously put aside: arrange them in a grid pattern and brush them with beaten egg. Bake for about one hour and a half, until the surface is golden brown. Leave to cool in the cake-tin for about 24 hours (but don't put it the fridge!). The filling will dry and firm up completely and the cake will show cracks all over its surface. Dust the *pastiera* with icing sugar and serve at room temperature. You can enjoy it over the next 4-5 days if you store it in the fridge.

The shapes of pasta

Agnolotti

Bucatini

Casonsei

Bavette

Cappelletti

Conchiglie

Farfalle

Garganelli

Gnocchi

Fusilli

Lasagne

Malloreddus

Orecchiette

Linguine

from "A" to "Z"

Pansotti

Paccheri

Penne

Pizzoccheri

Quadrucci

Ravioli

Rigatoni

Reginette

Ruote

Tagliatelle

Tortellini

Spaghetti

Spaghetti integrali

Ziti

Cheese and egg croquettes

500 g grated semi-mature cow milk cheese,
4 eggs, 500 g tomato pulp, 1 clove garlic,
1 onion, 1 green pepper, parsley,
oil for frying, salt.

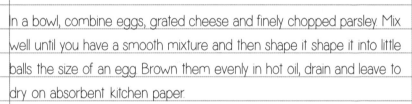

In a bowl, combine eggs, grated cheese and finely chopped parsley. Mix well until you have a smooth mixture and then shape it shape it into little balls the size of an egg. Brown them evenly in hot oil, drain and leave to dry on absorbent kitchen paper.

Prepare the sauce: chop the garlic, the onion and the pepper, sauté and add the tomato pulp and a pinch of salt. Cook for 20 minutes over medium heat. Add the croquettes to the tomato sauce, bring to a rolling boil and then lower the heat and leave to cook for about 10 minutes over low heat, so that the croquettes will get softer and tastier. Remove from heat, arrange on a serving dish and serve as an appetizer or second course.

For the sagne: 500 g flour, salt.
For the sauce: 600 g cicerchie (azure blue sweet peas),
80 g ham fat, 350 peeled tomatoes,
1 bunch basil and parsley, 2 cloves garlic, 1 onion,
1 red hot chili pepper, grated pecorino cheese,
extra-virgin olive oil, salt.

Sagne a pezze with cicerchie

(short broken pieces of lasagna with azure blue sweet peas)

Steep the sweet peas for at least 48 hours - rinse and change the water twice or three times a day. Rinse the peas carefully and boil them in salted water, adding a clove of garlic. Bring the water to a boil, then lower the heat and continue cooking the pea soup for half an hour. In the meantime, prepare the *sagne a pezze* (short broken pieces of lasagna) by adding some water to the flour and kneading thoroughly until you have a firm, smooth dough. Form a ball, cover with a cloth and let it sit for about 30 minutes. Sprinkle flour over a work surface, roll out the dough into a thin sheet (about 2 mm) and cut it into small oblique stripes about 4 cm wide. You will obtain small irregular rhombuses.

Chop the onion finely, crush the garlic, the basil and the parsley and sauté all the ingredients in a saucepan together with the ham fat chopped into small cubes. Add the tomatoes and the red hot chili pepper and simmer for15 minutes, then add this mixture to the sweet peas soup. Bring a pot of salted water to a rolling boil, cook the *sagne* and drain when al dente. Add the pasta to the sweet peas soup and leave to cook for five further minutes. Remove from heat, drizzle with olive oil and grated pecorino cheese. Serve hot.

For the maccheroni alla chitarra (this pasta takes its name from the guitar-like kitchen tool used to cut the dough):
500 g flour, 4 eggs.
For the sauce: 800 g peeled tomatoes, 150 g minced lamb meat, 150 g minced pork, 1 small onion, 1 carrot, grated Parmesan or pecorino cheese, 40 g butter, salt, pepper.
For the meatballs: 500 g ground beef, 3 eggs, 4 tablespoon grated Parmesan, parsley, ground nutmeg, salt, butter.

Prepare the maccheroni: mix the flour with the eggs and knead thoroughly until you have a smooth dough, then roll out the dough to thin sheets and use the *chitarra* to cut the maccheroni, by pressing the dough against the wires. Leave the maccheroni to dry on a tray sprinkled with flour and prepare the meat sauce. Peel the onion and the carrot, then chop them finely and sauté in a saucepan with the butter. Add the minced meat, stir well and cook for a few minutes before adding the peeled tomatoes. Season with salt and pepper, and simmer over moderate heat. Prepare the meatballs: in a bowl, mix the ground beef, the eggs, the grated Parmesan, the minced parsley, a pinch of nutmeg and a pinch of salt. Form tiny little balls (0,5 cm diameter), and cook in a saucepan with a little butter. Add the meatballs to the meat sauce and stir well. Cook the pasta in boiling salted water, drain when al dente and add the sauce. Sprinkle with grated cheese and serve.

Maccheroni alla chitarra with meat sauce

La **mugnaia**

(miller's pasta)

For the pasta: 250 g extra-fine flour,
250 g durum wheat flour, 1 egg.
For the sauce: 500 g pork (with its bone) and mutton or lamb
meat, 1 l tomato puree, ½ carrot, ½ pepper, ½ onion,
1 glass white wine, extra-virgin olive oil, salt.
Grated pecorino or Parmesan cheese.

Chop the onion, the carrot and the pepper and sauté in a saucepan. Add the meat, leave to brown and then pour some white wine. Simmer for 15 minutes, adding more white wine if necessary. Pour the tomato puree, season with salt and simmer over low heat for about one hour, until the sauce is thick and savoury. Prepare the dough for the pasta: mix the two kinds of flour and make a well on a work surface, add the egg and add some water (about 280 ml). Knead thoroughly until you have a smooth and firm dough. Leave to sit for about half an hour, then divide the dough into small portions (about 50 g each) and roll them into little strings (1 cm diameter), to be flattened with the palm of your hands. Cook the strings of pasta in plenty of boiling salted water for about 8 minutes, strain and mix with the meat sauce. Sprinkle generously with grated Parmesan or pecorino cheese and serve hot.

Bocconotti frentani

For 10 bocconotti (literally, 'mouthful', or 'bites')
For the pastry: 200 g extra-fine flour,
4 egg yolks and 1 egg white, 100 g sugar,
50 ml extra-virgin olive oil, the zest of ½ lemon,
1 glass aurum (brandy based liqueur flavoured with oranges)
or alchermes (Italian liqueur with a very aromatic flavor).
For the filling: 100 g sugar, 100 g chocolate,
100 g ground toasted almonds, 1 cinnamon stick, 2 egg yolks.
Decoration: icing sugar

Prepare the filling: boil half a litre of water with the sugar and the cinnamon stick for half an hour, then pass through a sieve, add the ground chocolate and cook for a further 30 minutes. Add the ground almonds, remove from heat and leave to cool. Add the egg yolks, beat the mixture with a whisk and bring to a rolling boil, until you have a dense, creamy mixture. Remove from heat and leave to cool while you prepare the pastry. Beat the egg yolks and the sugar with a whisk. In a different bowl, whisk the egg white to stiff peaks and fold in the egg yolks. Add the olive oil, the lemon zest and a glass of *aurum*. Mix well all the ingredients, slowly add the flour and knead thoroughly until you have a soft, smooth dough. Roll it out to a sheet with a rolling pin on a work surface sprinkled with flour. Cut out disks of dough and place them on the *bocconotti* pastry moulds, previously greased. Fill each *bocconotti* with the creamy mixture and top with a disc of dough. Bake in a pre-heated oven (180 °C) for 20 minutes, until the little cakes are golden brown. Garnish with icing sugar.

Arrosticini

(grilled lamb skewers, traditional dish from Abruzzo)

1 kg lamb, mutton,
sheep fat, salt, pepper.
Home-made bread, extra-virgin olive oil.

Cut the lamb into pieces (1-2 cm cubes), thread them into skewers 25-30 cm long, alternating fat pieces with lean pieces. Sprinkle with salt and pepper. Prepare the *furnacella* (a brazier with a typically elongated shape) using charcoals or embers. Grill the *arrosticini* directly over coals, turning them over until their outside is browned and crisp. Serve immediately, wrapping them in tinfoil or paper cornets, and eat with homemade bread drizzled with olive oil.

Bruschetta

Home-made bread (a loaf), tomatoes,
extra-virgin olive oil, garlic, basil, salt, pepper.

Cut the bread into slices with a thickness of about 1,5 cm. Toast the bread slices over a wood fire; alternatively you can grill them in the kitchen oven. When the bread slices are well toasted, lay them on a serving dish and rub one side with a clove of garlic cut in two, sprinkle with salt and drizzle with olive oil.

Alternatively you can prepare a tasty variation by chopping fresh tomatoes in small cubes, removing the seeds and the extra water and spreading a layer of tomatoes on top of your bruschetta. Season with salt and pepper and drizzle with extra-virgin olive oil, add some crushed basil and serve.

1 kg potatoes, 3 eggs,
150 g grated Parmesan,
50 g grated pecorino cheese, breadcrumbs,
1 mozzarella the size of a fist,
oil for frying, salt, pepper.

Steam or boil the potatoes for 10-15 minutes, then peel them and mash them well. Add the eggs, a pinch of salt, the grated cheese, a pinch of salt and pepper and mix well all the ingredients. Chop the mozzarella into small cubes. Divide the potato mixture into evenly sized small portions and form each one into a sausage shape about 6 cm long. Stuff each croquette with a mozzarella cube, close it and lay on a tray.

Heat some frying oil in a saucepan and brown evenly the potato croquettes. Drain, leave to dry on absorbent paper and serve hot.

Potato croquettes

500 g rice, 180 g butter, 1 onion, 100 g grated Parmesan, ground nutmeg, stock, 100 g raw ham, 50 g chicken giblets, 50 g lamb sweetbread, 50 g ground beef, 50 g dried mushrooms, 1 glass white wine, all-purpose flour, 1 egg, breadcrumbs, oil for frying, salt, pepper.

Supplì alla romana

(stuffed rice balls, Roman style)

Prepare a *risotto* with the rice, hot stock, 100 g of butter and the grated Parmesan. Retire from heat when al dente and turn it out onto on a marble work surface to cool. In a pot, cook the finely sliced onion with the remaining butter, add the raw ham finely chopped, the ground beef, the giblets and the sweetbread. Season with salt and pepper, pour the wine and simmer until reduced. Add a pinch of flour, three or four tablespoons of water and cook over medium-low heat until the sauce is dense and savoury. When the sauce is done, remove from heat and leave to cool.

With a spoon, make egg-shaped portions of the rice. Make an indentation in the centre of each one and place a teaspoon of filling in the centre of each ball of rice. Roll each ball in the flour, dip it in beaten egg and roll in the breadcrumbs, so that it is completely coated, and set aside.

In a large pot, heat the olive oil over high heat until it is almost smoking in batches. Fry the rice balls in the hot oil until they are golden brown, remove with a slotted spoon and allow to drain on paper towels. Serve hot.

1 kg chicory, 2 potatoes, 2-3- ripe tomatoes,
mint leaves, 1 red hot chili pepper,
2-3 cloves garlic, 1 onion,
4 eggs (optional), 2 fillet salted
codfish, stale bread,
extra-virgin olive oil, salt.

Acquacotta

('cooked water' soup)

Peel and chop the potatoes, coarsely slice the onion, chop and seed the tomatoes, peel and crush the garlic, crush the red hot chili pepper and cut the codfish fillets. In a large earthenware pot, stew all the ingredients with about a litre of water. Cover the pot and leave to cook for about an hour.

In a separate pot, cook the chicory with some mint leaves.

While the soup comes to the boil, place a slice of toasted bread in each soup plate. Ladle the soup over the bread slices, season with salt and top with the chicory, the potatoes, the codfish - and, if you like, the poached eggs. Leave to rest, pour off the excess liquid, drizzle with olive oil and serve.

Place the grated pecorino and plenty of freshly ground black pepper
in a large steel serving bowl.
Boil the spaghetti in salted hot water and drain when al dente,
putting aside some of the cooking water. Use this water to moist the
pecorino, then transfer the spaghetti to the serving bowl
and mix well before serving, adding some drops of olive oil.

Spaghetti cacio and pepper

500 g spaghetti, 250 g grated pecorino
romano cheese, extra-virgin olive oil, salt,
freshly ground black pepper.

"Cacio" is a dialectal name for cheese.
This traditional dish includes for cheese
only Pecorino Romano, that is a hard,
salty cheese made of sheep milk

360 g spaghetti, 200 cheek lard or bacon,
3 egg yolks, 4 tablespoons grated pecorino romano cheese,
4 tablespoons extra-virgin olive oil,
salt, freshly ground pepper.

Cut the cheek lard into small strips (or dice the bacon) and brown in a pan with olive oil for about 5 minutes over moderate heat. Remove from the heat and put aside. In a bowl, beat the egg yolks with two tablespoons of pecorino, a pinch of salt and plenty of freshly ground pepper.
Boil the spaghetti in plenty of hot salted water and drain it when al dente, keeping aside some of the cooking water. Transfer to the pan containing the crunchy cheek lard (or bacon), add the yolks and mix well all the ingredients. If the spaghetti looks too sticky you can add a couple of tablespoons of its own cooking water. Sprinkle with the grated pecorino and serve hot.
There are several variations to this dish. You can add the egg whites to the spaghetti: in that case you should sauté the pasta and its sauce over high heat for a further 3 minutes.

"Alla carbonara" means Charcol burner's style. It is commonly tributed to "Carbonari" a secret society in the age of the italian unification.

Spaghetti alla carbonara

Bucatini alla matriciana

(Roman style bucatini)

360 g bucatini (type of spaghetti),
150 g cheek lard (or streaky bacon),
500 very ripe, fresh tomatoes (or canned peeled tomatoes),
½ onion, 50 g grated pecorino cheese, ½ glass dry white wine,
4 tablespoons extra-virgin olive oil,
½ red hot chili pepper flakes, salt.

Cut the lard into small dices and slice the onion. Warm the olive oil in a large sauce pan over medium heat, add the onion and lard and cook slowly, until onions are soft and translucent and the pancetta fat is rendered. Pour the wine and simmer until reduced. Blanch the tomatoes, peel them and chop into small cubes, then add to the onion and lard, sprinkle with hot red pepper flakes and season with salt and pepper. Simmer and reduce the sauce over medium heat for about 15-20 minutes.

In the meantime, bring to a boil a pot of salted water and cook the *bucatini*. Drain when al dente, transfer to a serving bowl and mix with the sauce. Sprinkle generously with grated pecorino cheese and serve immediately.

400 g spaghetti, 50 g bacon,
80 g tuna fish, canned in oil, 2 cloves of garlic,
200 g porcino mushrooms,
3 tablespoons extra-virgin olive oil, salt, pepper.

"Alla carrettiera" means "cart driver's style" because this dish was easy to make and to transport for people whose job was to travel long distances by cart.

Spaghetti alla carrettiera

Wash and clean the mushrooms, cut them into thin slices and sauté in a saucepan with the diced bacon and the garlic, previously crushed. Remove the garlic after a couple of minutes, season with salt and pepper, stirring with a wooden spoon. Open the tuna can, strain it and add the tuna fish to the mushrooms. Cook for a further ten minutes over moderate heat.
Cook the spaghetti in plenty of boiling salted water, drain when al dente and add to the sauce. Stir well and serve.

1kg spring lamb, rosemary,
3-4 potatoes, lard, extra-virgin olive oil,
salt, pepper.

Wash and pat dry the meat. Cut slits in the lamb with a fine-bladed knife, and fill them with rosemary sprigs. Spread it with lard, season with salt and pepper and place in a roasting tin, previously greased with lard. Arrange the peeled and chopped potatoes around it, drizzle with olive oil and place in a pre-heated oven (180 °C). During cooking, turn the lamb and the potatoes over with a wooden spoon. Leave to cook until all is well browned and the potatoes are soft and savoury.

Cut the meat into pieces, arrange on a serving dish and serve.

Roast spring lamb

Saltimbocca alla romana

"Saltimbocca" mean "that jumps into mouth" because this meat so cooked is very tasty!

8 thin slices of veal, 8 slices Parma ham, 8 sage leaves, all-purpose flour, 1 glass dry white wine, 4 tablespoons extra-virgin olive oil, salt, pepper.

Dredge the veal in the flour, shaking off the excess. Place a slice of Parma ham and a leaf of sage in the centre of each cutlet and weave a toothpick in and out of the veal to secure the prosciutto and sage. Heat the oil (or butter, if you prefer) in a large skillet over medium flame. Put the veal in the pan, cook for 3 minutes to crisp it up and then flip the veal over and sauté the other side for 2 minutes, until golden. Add the wine to the pan, cover and leave to cook for 10 minutes, turning the *saltimbocca* only once. Season with salt and pepper and serve immediately with the cooking juices.

Puntarelle with anchovies

400 g puntarelle (chicory sprouts), 2 cloves garlic,
4 salted anchovy fillets, 2 tablespoons vinegar
(or aromatic vinegar), the juice of 1 lemon,
½ glass extra-virgin olive oil, salt, pepper.
If you like spicy food, you can add 1 a teaspoon of
hot red pepper flakes.

Prepare the oil dip: in the bowl of a food processor, combine the garlic, anchovies, vinegar, salt and pepper (and hot red pepper flakes, if you like spicy food). Star the machine and slowly drizzle in the oil, until you have a creamy sauce. If you don't have a food processor, chop finely the ingredients and blend them stirring with a fork. Leave to sit while you prepare the chicory sprouts. Wash carefully with cold running water the chicory heads, remove the tougher outer leaves and chop the tender inner leaves. Scrape the roots and remove the tougher part. Cut the *puntarelle* lengthwise into very thin strips. You may also use a potato peeler to get thinner strips, or a special kitchen tool called 'taglia-*puntarelle*'. Put the *puntarelle* into a bowl of cold water mixed with lemon juice for about an hour. This way they will curl up and lose their bitter flavour. Drain the chicory, place it in a salad bowl and dress with the oil dip. Mix well, leave to rest for half an hour and serve. *Puntarelle* can be served as an appetizer. Alternatively, you can add a spoonful of water, sauté them for 10-15 minutes, and then mix with pasta.

Artichokes alla giudia
(Sephardic style artichokes)

Roman artichokes, lemons,
extra-virgin olive oil, pepper.

Trim the outer leaves and the stems of each artichoke, then wash, drain and dry them. With a peeler, peel away the darker part of each leaf. Leave the artichokes in a bowl with water and the juice of the lemons for about ten minutes. If you walk around a typical Italian street market, you'll probably see buckets full of water near the fruit and vegetables stalls, where artichokes and lemon halves float freely: these artichokes are traditionally prepared by old ladies - stallholders' mothers, or mothers-in-law - usually sitting in a corner trimming vegetables and chatting loudly.

Drain and dry the artichokes; using your hands flatten the artichokes to the shape of a flower, sprinkle with salt and pepper and leave to sit for 5-10 minutes. In a casserole, heat a large quantity of olive oil (enough to cover the artichokes); when it's warm add the artichokes, leaving to cook for no more than 10 minutes. Remove from the pan, leave to cool for 15 minutes. In a deep saucepan, heat a large quantity of olive oil over a high heat, sprinkle the artichokes with water (this will crisp the leaves) and add them to the pan, one by one and stem up. When the leaves have flattened out completely and the artichokes are crisp and golden brown, drain and arrange on absorbent paper. Serve immediately.

"Alla giudia" means Jewish-style because this dish was a speciality of the Roman Ghetto.

Rigatoni alla norcina

360 g rigatoni, 400 g sausage, skinned and sliced, 2 eggs,
20 g black truffle, 2 tablespoons grated pecorino cheese,
2 tablespoons grated Parmesan, ½ glass single cream,
½ glass dry white wine, 4 tablespoons extra-virgin olive oil,
ground nutmeg, salt, pepper.

In a pan, heat some olive oil and brown the sausage. Pour some wine and cook for ten minutes. In a bowl, beat the eggs with a pinch of salt and pepper, a pinch of ground nutmeg, the cheese and the single cream. Mix well all the ingredients. Cook the rigatoni in plenty of salted water, drain when al dente and transfer to the pan with the sausage. Add the egg mixture, stir well and leave to sit for a couple of minutes. Remove from the heat, sprinkle with grated (or thinly sliced) black truffle and serve immediately.

"Rigatoni" is a form of tube-shaped pasta, normally ridged. "Riga" in Italian means "line".

"Alla norcina" means Norcia-style. Norcia is a pleasant, walled city in Umbria, famous for the pork products. The shop of a pork butcher any where in Italy is called "norcineria".

Bean soup

300 pinto beans, 1 onion,
1 stick of celery, 1 clove
garlic, 1 bunch parsley,
1 bunch basil, 2 ripe
tomatoes, toasted bread slices,
extra-virgin olive oil,
salt, pepper.

Leave the beans to soak for 12 hours, then drain and cook in plenty of salted water for one hour. Drain the beans and put aside the cooking water. Finely chop the onion, celery and garlic, and sauté in a saucepan with 4 tablespoons of olive oil for 5 minutes. Add the beans and a spoonful or two of their cooking water. Add the tomatoes, previously peeled and chopped, and cook for half an hour adding some more cooking water if necessary. Season with pepper and add the crushed parsley and basil. Prepare toasted bread slices, arrange them in a soup tureen and pour a spoonful or two of soup over the bread slices. Lay some more bread slices and pour over some more soup. Continue to add the layers until all the soup is used up. Drizzle with olive oil and serve.

Sausage

and shallot frittata

4 eggs, 200 g sausage, 4 shallots,
1 rosemary sprig, 1 thyme sprig, 100 g sweet pecorino cheese,
4 tablespoons extra-virgin olive oil, salt.

Once you've eliminated the roots, peel the shallots and chop into thin slices, then sauté in a saucepan with olive oil and add the peeled and chopped sausage. Cook for 10 minutes, then scoop shallot and sausage with a skimmer and put aside to cool. In a bowl, beat the eggs and season with salt and pepper, then add the crushed parsley and thyme. Add the sausage and the cubed pecorino cheese to the egg mixture, then pour everything back into the saucepan you used to fry the sausage and the shallot. Cook over low heat until the frittata pulls away from the sides slightly, flip it over and finish cooking. Cut into slices and serve immediately.

Olive

40 large green olives, 300 g breadcrumbs,
100 g minced beef, 100 g minced chicken, 100 g minced
pork, 100 grated pecorino cheese or grated Parmesan
cheese, 100 g all-purpose flour, 50 g Parma ham,
2 eggs, 1 carrot, 1 stick of celery, 1 onion,
1 tablespoon peeled tomatoes, 80 g extra-virgin olive oil,
ground nutmeg, salt, pepper.

Pit the olives carefully. Mix the three kinds of ground meat and chop the Parma ham, then brown in a saucepan with a little olive oil. Add the vegetables, previously chopped, and the peeled tomatoes. Season with salt and pepper and cook until the vegetables are done. Remove from the heat, remove the vegetables from the mixture and leave the meat to cool. In a bowl, mix the grated Parmesan, the ground nutmeg, two egg yolks, one egg white and the meat. Stir until you have a smooth mixture, season with salt and use this mixture to stuff the olives. Prepare three bowls: the first one for the flour, the second one for the egg white (previously beaten until stiff) and the third one for the breadcrumbs. Cover the olives in flour, then dip them in the egg white and finally roll them in breadcrumbs. Leave to sit for about half an hour, and then fry in hot oil until they're evenly golden brown. Lay on absorbent paper, serve hot.

all'ascolana

"All'ascolana" means Ascoli-style. Ascoli is a beautiful city in the Marches.

Brodetto *alla fanese*
(fish soup Fano style)

1,5 kg mixed fish from Adriatic Sea (cuttlefish, squids,
mussels, clams, dogfish, ray, monkfish, rockfish,
anglerfish, mullets, mantis prawn, etc.),
4 tablespoons tomato paste, 4 slices homemade bread,
1 onion, 1 clove garlic, 1 bunch parsley, 80 ml
extra-virgin olive oil, ½ glass vinegar, salt, pepper.

Clean and scale all the fish, de-beard mussels and clams.
Wash in cold, running water and dry. Take a wide two-
handle saucepan, heat some olive oil and sauté the finely sliced
onion and the crushed garlic. Add the tomato paste previously
diluted in vinegar, two glasses of warm water or fish stock, season
with salt and pepper. Simmer for a few minutes, and then add the
fish according to their cooking time. Start with the cuttlefish, chop
into large pieces, and then add the mussels and the clams. Cook for
ten minutes, then add mantis prawns, dogfish, ray, monkfish, rockfish,
anglerfish and so on. Finish with the more tender fish pieces at the
top, like prawns and mullets. Cook for a further 10 minutes over
low heat, shaking the pan every now
and then. Ladle the soup in warmed
soup bowls, with toast bread slices
on the side. Sprinkle with
chopped parsley and serve hot.

Vincisgrassi

400 g egg lasagna, 300 g ground beef,
300 g ground pork, 300 g chicken giblets,
(heart, liver, kidneys, gizzards), 1 onion, 1 carrot,
1 stick of celery, 1 cup of tomato pulp,
2 tablespoons tomato puree, 50 g Parmesan, 1 l milk,
50 g butter, 100 g bacon fat, 1 glass red wine,
4 tablespoons extra-virgin olive oil, salt and pepper.

When you clean the chicken giblets, the liver needs to be separated from the gallbladder. The gallbladder contains bile - an extremely bitter green fluid - and must be handled carefully because the bile can contaminate the meat and cause it to be inedible. Rinse the giblets accurately with cold water and pat dry with a paper towel and chop finely. Chop the bacon fat, the onion, the carrot and the celery and sauté them in a saucepan with butter. Add the finely chopped chicken giblets, the ground beef and the ground pork, brown them for about ten minutes while stirring, then pour in the white wine. As soon as it has evaporated, add the tomato pulp and the tomato puree diluted in warm water. Cover and simmer over low heat for about an hour and a half. Season with salt and pepper halfway through the cooking. Stir from time to time, adding hot stock if necessary, in order to keep the minced meat under about 5 cm of liquid. Towards the end of the cooking time, uncover the saucepan to evaporate the extra liquid. Boil the lasagna strips in plenty of salted water. Add a tablespoon of olive oil to the water, so the lasagna strips won't stick together. When the lasagna is half-cooked, drain and let dry on clean cotton cloths. Butter an ovenproof dish and spread a layer of meat sauce and grated Parmesan, then a layer of lasagna, béchamel (rather fluid), Parmesan. Repeat the layers - béchamel, meat sauce, béchamel, Parmesan - until all the ingredients are used up, ending with a layer of meat sauce covered with béchamel and Parmesan. Cook in a pre-heated oven at 180 °C for about 30 minutes. Serve hot.

The different loaves and rolls

Pane Toscano

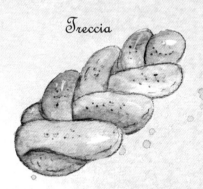

Treccia

Panini al Latte

Pane Integrale

Pane Pugliese

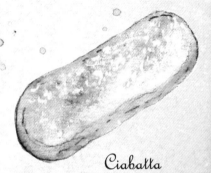

Ciabatta

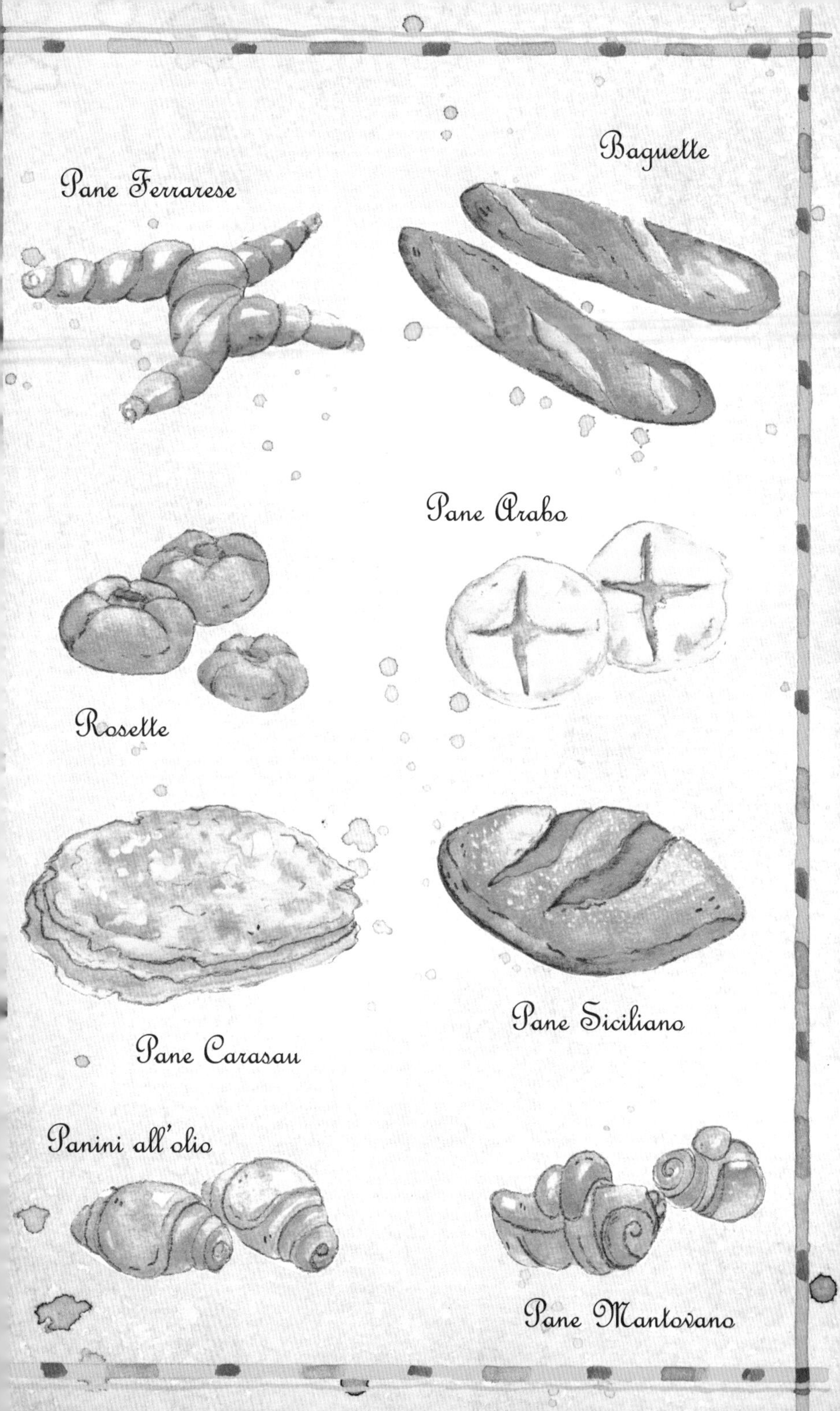

Pane Ferrarese

Baguette

Pane Arabo

Rosette

Pane Carasau

Pane Siciliano

Panini all'olio

Pane Mantovano

Chicken in potacchio
(braised chicken)

1 chicken, 2 tomatoes, 2 cloves garlic, 1 sprig rosemary,
1 onion, 1 glass dry white wine, 50 ml extra-virgin olive oil,
salt, pepper.

Clean the chicken, rinse it and cut it into chunks. Finely chop the onion and crush the garlic, then sauté in a deep saucepan. Add the chicken and brown it stirring from time to time. Pour the white wine, season with salt and pepper and simmer until reduced. Add the rosemary and the tomatoes, previously peeled and chopped into small cubes. Cover with a lid and cook over low heat for half an hour, stirring from time to time. Serve hot.

"In potacchio" means cooked in a pot with flavours.

Rabbit in potacchio

1 rabbit (about 1 kg, cleaned and cut into chunks),
5 garlic cloves, 2 sprigs rosemary, 100 g lard or bacon,
1 glass dry white wine, extra-virgin olive oil,
white wine vinegar, salt, pepper.

Wash and dry the rabbit pieces, and then soak in water and vinegar for a few hours. Drain and pat dry. In a casserole, sauté a clove of garlic and the cubed lard (or bacon) in a few spoons of olive oil. Add the rabbit chops and brown all over, season with salt and pepper, add the rosemary and the crushed garlic, pour the wine, cover with a lid and cook for about 30-40 minutes over moderate heat. Remove the casserole from heat and serve hot.

Panzanella

400 stale Tuscan bread,
4 ripe tomatoes,
2 red onions from Certaldo (or shallots),
basil, vinegar,
extra-virgin olive oil, salt.

Soak the bread in water to soften for about 15 minutes, and then squeeze it and crumble it in a bowl. Chop the tomatoes into small cubes, finely slice the onions and crush the basil. Add the ingredients to the bread. Season with salt, sprinkle with vinegar and drizzle with very little olive oil. Cover the bowl, leave to rest in the fridge for about half an hour and then add a sprinkle of olive oil, mix lightly and serve. You may accompany the *panzanella* with canned tuna fish in oil and a couple of hard-boiled eggs.

Crostoni

Stale Tuscan bread in slices,
2 bunches Tuscan kale, 2 cloves garlic,
extra-virgin olive oil, salt, freshly ground black pepper.

Wash and trim the kale leaves, and eliminate the stems. Cook in boiling water, drain and squeeze out the excess water, and then chop finely. Heat some oil in a pan and sauté the crushed garlic and the kale for 3 minutes. Season with salt and remove from the heat.

Toast the bread and rub the slices with a clove of garlic. Spread the kale on the toasted bread, sprinkle with freshly ground pepper and serve.

Alternatively, you can sauté half a hot red pepper with the garlic and kale. In that case you won't need to sprinkle with pepper.

with Tuscan Kale

Stale Tuscan bread, cut into thin slices,
400 canellini (dried white beans, also known as Great
Northern), ½ Savoy cabbage, 5 leaves Tuscan kale, 2 carrots,
1 stick of celery, 1 onion, 2 courgettes, 2 ripe tomatoes
(or canned peeled tomatoes), 2 potatoes, 1 bunch parsley,
5 leaves chard, 100 g rigatino (bacon),
extra-virgin olive oil, salt, pepper.

Ribollita is a typical Tuscan dish: there are many versions of this recipe, but the main ingredients are stale Tuscan bread, white beans and black cabbage. First of all, prepare a bean soup (see '*fagioli all'uccelletto*'). While the beans cook, heat the oil in a large stock pot and sauté the diced onion, carrot, celery, parsley and bacon. Add the diced potatoes, courgettes and tomatoes, then add the thinly sliced Savoy cabbage, the black cabbage and the chard. Add about a litre of water and leave to cook for one hour. Pass the beans and their liquid through a food mill and add this mixture to the vegetables. Leave to cook for about 15 minutes, stirring constantly. In a tureen, arrange layers of bread and pour the soup over them. Leave to sit for about 10 minutes, drizzle with olive oil and serve.

In Siena the *ribollita* ('re-boiled') is also called 'the soup' par excellence: it owes its name to the way it is prepared and then re-heated in an earthenware pot over very low heat.

Ribollita (Tuscan soup)

Spaghetti with garlic, olive oil and chili pepper

360 g spaghetti, 2 cloves garlic,
1 bunch parsley,
grated Parmesan,
4 tablespoons extra-virgin olive oil,
½ coffee spoon red chili pepper flakes, salt.

In a small pan, heat some olive oil and add the crushed garlic and the pepper flakes. Brown for a couple of minutes over very low heat, stirring carefully. Season with salt. Cook the spaghetti in plenty of hot salted water, drain when al dente and season with the oil. You can remove the garlic if you want a milder sauce. Sprinkle with finely chopped parsley and grated Parmesan. Serve hot.

400 g freshly home-made pappardelle,
1 kg g ground lean wild boar meat,
3 big sausages or 300 g ground pork,
500 g tomato pulp or canned peeled tomatoes,
1 onion, 1 carrot, 1 stick of celery, 1 bay leaf,
1 glass of red wine, extra-virgin olive oil, pepper, salt.

Pappardelle with wild boar

Pappardelle are similar to *tagliatelle*, only slightly wider (about 3 cm). Peel and wash the onion, the carrot and the celery; chop them finely and sauté the mixture in a little olive oil. Add the tomato pulp and the bay leaf, and when the mixture of chopped vegetables starts browning add the ground meat. Pork makes the sauce juicier, as wild boar meat is rather lean.
Season with salt and pepper, brown the meat for a few minutes and then pour the red wine. Allow to evaporate, add the tomato pulp and simmer over low heat for at least one hour. Season with salt before removing from heat. Boil the *pappardelle* in a lot of salted hot water, drain when al dente and pour into the pan containing the sauce. Sprinkle with grated cacio cheese and serve.

Ravioli della val Pusteria

*For the pasta dough: 250 g of rye flour, 250 g of wheat flour,
150 g of butter, 2 eggs and salt.
For the filling: 500 g of spinach, 150 g of ricotta cheese,
a ¼ onion, a spoonful of grated grana Trentino cheese,
nutmeg, butter, salt and pepper.
For the condiment: butter and grated grana cheese.*

Make a smooth and firm dough, kneading the two kinds of flour for quite a long tie with the egg, the room temperature softened butter and a little salt. Form a dough roll and leave the pasta to rest, cover with a damp tea towel for at least an hour. In the meantime start to get the filling ready. Wash and boil the spinach using only the water left from washing it, drain and squeeze well. Gently brown a shopped onion with the butter in a pan and then add the spinach and sauté for a few minutes. With the heat switched off add the sieved ricotta cheese, a spoonful of grated grana cheese, pepper and nutmeg. Use a rolling pin to roll out the pasta on a flour-dusted flat surface to make a very thin sheet of dough. Cut out circles of 6 cm diameter and put a teaspoon of filling in the middle of each. Close the ravioli envelopes in half moon shapes that are tightly closed at the edges by the pressure of your fingers and then also with the prongs of a fork. Boil the ravioli in plenty of salted boiling water. Just a few minutes cooking will be enough. Drain with a skimmer ladle and serve with the addition on the plate of melted butter and grated grana cheese.

Tortellini are a stuffed pasta made in several different shapes.

Potato tortelli

For the pasta: 400 g flour, 4 eggs, salt.
For the filling: ½ kg russet potatoes, boiled and mashed,
1 ripe tomato, 2 cloves garlic, parsley, grated Parmesan,
butter, 4-5 tablespoons extra-virgin olive oil,
ground nutmeg, salt, pepper.

Crush the garlic and parsley and sauté in a pan with olive oil. Blanch the tomato, chop it into small cubes and add to the pan. Add the mashed potatoes, two tablespoons of grated Parmesan, 10-15 g of butter, a pinch of ground nutmeg, salt and pepper. Prepare the pasta: form a well with the flour, add the eggs and a pinch of salt and knead well until you obtain a soft, smooth dough.

Leave to rest for a while under a cloth, then roll it out to a thin sheet of pastry and cut out circles of about 6 centimeters in diameter. Place a tablespoon of potato mixture in the centre of each circle, fold them over and press firmly the edges to seal the *tortelli*

Bring a pot of salted water to a boil, cook the *tortelli* for about 3-4 minutes, then drain and season with a tasty meat sauce (like beef and pork sauce). Sprinkle with grated Parmesan and serve.

1 porterhouse steak or T-bone steak
(about 1 kg, preferably young beef),
herbs and spices for seasoning
(rosemary, sage, marjoram, dill),
4 tablespoons extra-virgin olive oil, salt, pepper.

Rinse and chop the herbs, then rub them all over the meat and leave in the fridge for 24 hours, allowing the seasoning to permeate the meat. Remove the steak from the fridge and keep at room temperature for a couple of hours before cooking. Make sure you don't sprinkle the meat with salt - this way the meat won't lose its juices before being cooked.
Place a grill pan over high heat and grill the steak for 5-7 minutes, then turn and grill the other side for 3-5 minutes. The meat is done (medium-rare) when you can remove it easily from the grill. Once removed from the heat, sprinkle the steak with salt and pepper and allow to rest for a few minutes before slicing. Carve the meat off the bone, slice the meat, sprinkle with salt and pepper, drizzle with olive oil and serve immediately with grilled potatoes, or sautéed onions and fennels.

Bistecca alla fiorentina

(Florentine style beefsteak)

1 kg tripe, 2 red onions,
2 carrots, 1 stick celery,
½ kg peeled tomatoes, grated Parmesan,
extra-virgin olive oil, salt, pepper.

Cut the tripe into very thin strips.
Chop the vegetables and sauté in a saucepan with olive oil
- you may also add some ground bacon.
Add the tripe and cook for half an hour,
stirring frequently to prevent sticking.
Add the peeled and diced tomatoes,
season with salt and pepper and simmer until reduced.
Serve hot, sprinkled with a lot of grated Parmesan.

Trippa
alla fiorentina

(Florentine style tripe)

300 g dogfish, 300 g rockfish (or monkfish, or tub gurnard), 300 g mullet, 350 g octopus, 350 g squid, 16 mullets, 300 g prawns, herbs (1 onion, 1 carrot, 1 stick of celery, 4 cloves of garlic, 4 sage leaves, parsley), 1 red pepper, 400 g peeled tomatoes, 1 tablespoon tomato paste, 1 glass red wine, 8 tablespoons extra-virgin olive oil, salt, pepper. 4 slices toasted bread, garlic.

Cacciucco *alla livornese*

(Livorno style fish soup)

Clean all the fish, remove the heads and put them aside. In a large pan, heat 4 tablespoons of oil and sauté two crushed garlic cloves, the red pepper and the sage leaves. Add the chopped octopus and the squids, previously sliced into rings. Pour the wine, cover and cook over a low heat for 15 minutes, stirring from time to time. Add the tomato paste, diluted in a couple of tablespoon of warm water. Leave to cook over a low heat. Chop the onion, carrot, celery and parsley and sauté in a saucepan with a little olive oil. Add the rockfish and the mullet (with their heads), a pinch of salt and the tomato pulp. Add a cup of water and simmer for 15-20 minutes, then remove from the pot all the fish and the vegetables, pass them through a sieve or through a food-mill and then add the mixture to the casserole containing the squid and the octopus. Put aside the cooking juices for later. When the octopus and the squids are nearly done, add the chopped dogfish, the shelled prawns and the mullets, previously de-bearded. Season with salt and pepper, and cook for a further 10 minutes. Sprinkle with pepper and serve in bowls, poured over slices of toasted bread rubbed with garlic.

500 g dried cannellini beans
(Great Northern or navy),
250 g tomato pulp, hot red
pepper flakes,
sage leaves, 2-3- cloves
garlic, extra-virgin olive oil,
salt, pepper.

Soak the beans for at least 12 hours in cold water, then drain and cook in a large saucepan for about 1 hour. In a saucepan, heat some olive oil and sauté the garlic, then add the sage leaves and remove from the heat. When it's nearly cold, put it back on the heat and add the cannellini beans with a spoonful of their cooking water. Season with salt and pepper, and sprinkle with hot red pepper flakes. Simmer for a few minutes, add the tomato pulp and continue cooking for about ten minutes. Serve hot. This is a traditional side dish from Maremma; in Italian, an *uccelletto* is a small bird, so to cook beans all'*uccelletto* means you'll use the same seasonings you would use for a small game bird, namely, tomato, garlic, and sage. People used to say '*gli uccelletti son scappati*' (the little birds are gone!) to indicate that the food was over!

Fagioli all'uccelletto
(white beans Tuscan style)

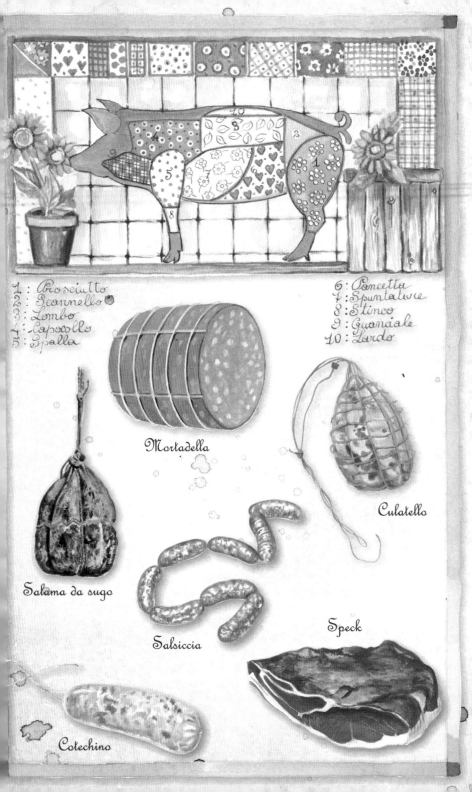

1 : Prosciutto
2 : Scannello
3 : Lombo
4 : Capocollo
5 : Spalla

6 : Pancetta
7 : Spuntature
8 : Stinco
9 : Guanciale
10 : Lardo

Mortadella

Culatello

Salama da sugo

Salsiccia

Speck

Cotechino

400 g extra-fine flour, 1 sachet baking powder, 200 g sugar, 120 g butter, 3 eggs, 1 egg yolk, 200 g unpeeled almonds, 1 sachet vanilla extract, salt, 2 tablespoons vin santo (or marsala wine).

Cantucci

(twice-baked cookies common in Tuscany)

Sieve the flour with the baking powder, the vanilla extract, a pinch of salt and the sugar. Make a well on a work surface and add the wine, the softened butter and the eggs. Mix well all the ingredients and knead thoroughly until you have a smooth, soft dough. Add the unpeeled almonds previously chopped. Form flat sausage shapes about 6 cm wide and 2 cm thick, lay them on a floured baking tray and brush them with egg yolk. Bake in a pre-heated oven (180 °C) for about half an hour, then leave to cool for a few minutes and cut into diagonal slices (about 2 cm wide) to obtain the classic *cantucci* shape. Put back the biscuits in the oven (100 °C) for a further 10 minutes, making sure you turn them over half way through the cooking process. Serve cool. *Cantucci* can be stored in glass jars.

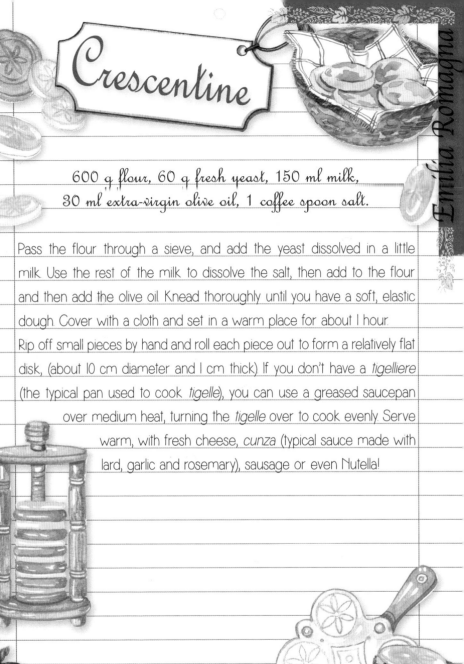

Crescentine

600 g flour, 60 g fresh yeast, 150 ml milk,
30 ml extra-virgin olive oil, 1 coffee spoon salt.

Pass the flour through a sieve, and add the yeast dissolved in a little milk. Use the rest of the milk to dissolve the salt, then add to the flour and then add the olive oil. Knead thoroughly until you have a soft, elastic dough. Cover with a cloth and set in a warm place for about 1 hour.

Rip off small pieces by hand and roll each piece out to form a relatively flat disk, (about 10 cm diameter and 1 cm thick) If you don't have a *tigelliere* (the typical pan used to cook *tigelle*), you can use a greased saucepan over medium heat, turning the *tigelle* over to cook evenly. Serve warm, with fresh cheese, *cunza* (typical sauce made with lard, garlic and rosemary), sausage or even Nutella!

nelle tigelle

300 g flour, 1,5 kg Swiss chard leaves or spinach, 1 onion, (or 2 shallots, or 2 spring onions, or 1 leek), 1 clove garlic, 1 sprig parsley, 200 g bacon, 100 grated Parmesan, 60 g butter, 1 egg yolk, extra-virgin olive oil, 1 glass mineral water, salt, pepper.

Erbazzone
(herb sandwich from Parma)

Make a well with the flour, add the butter, a pinch of salt and mineral water. Knead thoroughly until you have a soft, smooth dough. Put aside to sit for a while. Prepare the filling: wash the chard leaves carefully, cook in boiling salted water for about 15-20 minutes. Drain squeeze out excess water and chop finely. Chop the bacon and sauté in a pan with olive oil, add the crushed garlic and the onion, finely chopped. Add the chard leaves and the chopped parsley, season with salt and pepper and cook for a few minutes, then remove from heat and leave to cool. Sprinkle with Parmesan and mix well. Grease a pizza pan (or a pie dish), then take the dough out of the fridge, divide it into two halves and roll out two rounds (one slightly bigger than the pizza pan). Fit the larger round of pastry into the pizza pan and spread the filling over the pastry. Top with the remaining sheet, fold the edges of the bigger sheet over the tart and crimp. Make slashes in the top of the crust and brush it with egg yolk. Bake in a pre-heated oven (180 °C) for about 30 minutes, then bake au gratin for a couple of minutes. Leave to cool and serve. If you prefer, you can prepare the *erbazzone* with a single sheet of pastry (no top); instead of Swiss chard leaves or spinaches you may use beet tops.

500 g flour,
100 g lard,
1 teaspoon baking soda,
½ teaspoon sugar, salt.

Piadina romagnola
(flatbread)

"Romagna" is a region of gentle hills between the River Po and Appennines. It slopes down to the Adriatic sea. It is appealing to tourists, as well as being famed for its culinary delights.

Make a well with the flour, add the lard, the baking soda, the sugar and the salt. Mix well, add a little water and knead thoroughly until you have a smooth, elastic dough. If you want a crispier *piadina*, you may add milk instead of water. Cover the dough with a cloth and leave to sit for several hours, then divide the dough into pieces the size of a fist, and roll them out to form rounds 4 mm thick. Place a grill-pan over medium heat and grill for 4 minutes each side. Remove the *piadina* from the grill to cool slightly and serve with a filling of ham or cheese.

350 g boned veal, 150 g bacon,
1 stick celery, 1 onion,
1 carrot, 2 bay leaves,
1 handful dried mushrooms,
2-3 peeled tomatoes,
ground cinnamon,
50 g butter,
2 tablespoons aromatic
vinegar from Modena,
salt, pepper.

Rinse the mushrooms and leave to soak in a bowl of lukewarm water. Cut the meat into small pieces and chop the onion, carrot and celery. Sauté the vegetables with some butter, add the minced bacon and brown for a few minutes, stirring frequently with a wooden spoon. Add the tomatoes, crushing them with a fork. Add the meat and sauté for a few minutes over moderate heat. Add the strained mushrooms, a pinch of cinnamon and the bay leaves. Season with salt, pepper and aromatic vinegar. Cover and cook for an hour over low heat, stirring occasionally.

Meat sauce with aromatic vinegar

Baked cannelloni

12 cannelloni (pasta shells).
For the filling: 100 g ground beef, 100 g ground veal,
80 g ground chicken, 80 g Bologna sausage, 60 g butter,
60 g grated Parmesan, salt.
For the béchamel: ½ l milk, 2 tablespoons all-purpose flour,
30 g butter, ground nutmeg, salt.
For topping: 20 g butter, 20 g grated Parmesan.

This recipe comes straight from my grandma's cookbook, but there are many more ways of preparing a delicious filling for your *cannelloni*: you can use different kinds of meat, including roast left-overs, spinach and other vegetables. As long as the ingredients are savoury and well-seasoned, the result will be a success! Bring to a boil a pot of salted water and cook the cannelloni. Drain when al dente, dip into a bowl of cool water to halt the cooking process and lay on a kitchen towel to dry. Prepare the béchamel (it must be quite dense and creamy), then prepare the sauce: sauté the meat in a pan with some butter and remove from heat when it's browned. Add some béchamel (a half of what you have prepared) and some grated Parmesan. Stuff the *cannelloni* with the meat sauce and lay them in a baking dish; cover with the béchamel, add the butter (previously cubed) and sprinkle with Parmesan. Bake in a pre-heated oven (180°) until brown golden.

Home-made
Pasta

300 g extra-fine flour,
200 g durum wheat flour,
3 eggs,
2 tablespoons
extra-virgin olive oil,
salt.

Mix the two types of flour on the breadboard. Make a well in the centre and blend in the eggs, the olive oil and a pinch of salt, mixing until a dough is formed. Knead thoroughly, adding a little lukewarm water, until you have a consistent, smooth dough. Cover with a cloth and leave to sit for half an hour in a warm place, then knead again. Roll out the dough into thin sheets with a rolling pin; you may also use a pasta-machine - in that case the pasta will have a smoother texture, less prone to hold onto sauce.

Leave the thin sheets of pasta to dry on a cloth for a couple of hours, then cut it into strips of the desired width.

Prepare the dough following the instructions for home-made pasta (previous page), and cut it into strips of the desired width in order to obtain *tagliatelle*, *pappardelle* or *tagliolini*. Roll up the sheet of dough to form a roll and cut it into thin perpendicular stripes: *pappardelle* are 1 cm wide (and slightly thicker), *tagliatelle* are 5 mm wide, and *tagliolini* are 1 mm wide.

Tagliatelle are delicious with meat sauce, peas, bladder campion, porcini mushroom or truffle sauce or simply melted butter. *Pappardelle* go well with meat sauces, especially game sauces, and *tagliolini* are usually cooked in hot meat stock.

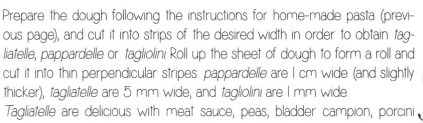

Tagliatelle, pappardelle and tagliolini

(home-made pasta from Romagna)

100 g extra-fine flour
and 1 egg per person.

Passatelli in hot meat stock

1,5 l meat stock, 4 eggs, 230 g grated Parmesan, 170 g breadcrumbs, 1 tablespoon all-purpose flour, ground nutmeg, salt.

Complete with: 100 g grated Parmesan.

In a bowl, combine the eggs, flour, grated Parmesan, breadcrumbs, a pinch of ground nutmeg, a pinch of salt. Traditionally, the *passatelli* were made with a special perforated and disc-shaped kitchen tool, but a food mill will work just as well. Transfer the cheese mixture to a food mill fitted with the large die. Turn the handle so that the mixture is forced through the mill on a floured breadboard. Cover with a cloth and leave to sit. Bring to the boil a pot of meat stock and cook the *passatelli* for one minute, then remove the pot from heat and leave to rest for 5 minutes before serving, sprinkled with grated Parmesan. In the past, women used to give the *passatelli* dough an elongated shape (salami-like) and cook it in hot meat stock. Then they would cut it into slices, place them in bowls and pour hot stock over.

"Passatelli" are a kind of pasta. The name means "passed them through" because they are made using a kind of potato press.

94

Strozzapreti alla boscaiola

(literally, 'priest-strangler', with porcini mushroom sauce)

For the dough: 350 g extra-fine flour, 1 egg white, salt.
For the sauce: 400 g fresh porcini mushrooms (or 80 g dried porcini), 1 clove garlic, 1 sprig parsley, 100 g ham, in one slice, 2 ripe tomatoes, 4 tablespoons single cream, 40 g butter (or 4 tablespoons extra-virgin olive oil), salt, freshly ground white pepper.

Make a well with the flour, add the egg white and a pinch of salt. Knead thoroughly, adding as much water as necessary to obtain a smooth, firm dough. Roll out the dough with a rolling pin to a very thin sheet (about 2 mm thick) and cut into squares (about 3 cm x 3 cm size). Wet your hands and roll the squares one by one forming little cylinders; lay them on the breadboard to dry.

In a pan, sauté the crushed garlic and the sliced mushrooms (if you use dried mushroom, steep in warm water for I hour, then drain and squeeze out e excess water), season with salt and simmer over medium heat for 10-15 minutes. Half way through the cooking, add the peeled and seeded tomatoes, the diced ham and the single cream. Stir well, add a little finely chopped parsley and remove from heat.

Bring to a boil a pot of salted water, cook the *strozzapreti* and drain when al dente (5-6 minutes). Transfer to the pan with the mushroom sauce, sprinkle with freshly ground white pepper, stir well and serve.

For the pastry: 400 g extra-fine flour, 4 eggs.
For the filling: 1 kg yellow pumpkin, 1 egg,
3 tablespoons grated Parmesan,
breadcrumbs, ground nutmeg, salt.
For the sauce: 100 g butter, sage leaves,
grated Parmesan.

Wash the pumpkin, chop into small pieces and remove the seeds. Bake in a very hot oven (200°-220 °C) for about half an hour. Scoop out the pulp and mash it in a bowl. Leave to cool and then add an egg, three tablespoons of grated Parmesan, a pinch of ground nutmeg, two pinches of salt and enough breadcrumbs to obtain a soft dough. Stir well, and add a pinch of sugar if you think the mixture is not sweet enough.

Prepare the pastry: combine the flour with the eggs, knead well until you have a soft, smooth dough. Roll out with a rolling pin to a thin sheet, leave to rest for about 15 minutes and cut out squares about 8 cm x 8 cm. Place a tablespoon of pumpkin filling in the centre of each square, fold the top left corner over and press the edges down. Now fold the diagonal side (with filling) over once, turn the pasta and cross the tails over each other. Cook the *cappellacci* for 5 minutes in plenty of boiling salted water, drain with a perforated spoon when the pasta is soft but not floppy.

Toss the pasta with the sauce made with melted butter, sage leaves and grated Parmesan. Serve immediately.

Pumpkin cappellacci
(stuffed pasta with pumpkin filling)

Stuffed courgettes

12 medium size courgettes, 50 g butter, 3 amaretti cookies (optional), 50 g breadcrumbs, 1 egg, 1 small onion, 1 tablespoon tomato paste, ½ stock cube, salt. Butter (for baking).

Trim and wash the courgettes and cut in half lengthwise. Scoop the pulp and grind it, put the courgettes aside for later.

Prepare the filling: in a pan, melt 40 g of butter and sauté the finely chopped onion. Add the tomato paste (previously diluted in half a glass of warm water), the stock cube and a pinch of salt. Stir the sauce, and then add the courgette pulp and the ground *amaretti* (optional). Stir and cook for about 10 minutes, then remove from heat.

In a pan, toast the breadcrumbs, then add them to the filling together with the grated Parmesan and the egg. Mix well with a wooden spoon.

Blanch the courgettes in boiling salted water, drain and arrange in a greased baking tray. Place a little of the filling into the hollowed-out part of each courgette, add some butter and bake in a pre-heated oven (180 °C) for about half an hour.

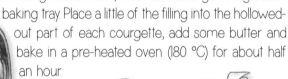

Prosciutto and melon

1 rather large ripe melon, 200 g of prosciutto crudo dolce, or uncooked cured ham, and salt (if desired).

Cut the chilled melon into slices and remove the seeds and peel. Place the prosciutto slices in the centre of the serving dish and around them the slices of melon. To taste add a little salt.

Tiramisù

500 g of mascarpone, 500g of Savoyard ladyfinger or Pavesini biscuits, 8 cups of coffee, 6 spoons of sugar and 4 eggs. To finish off: bitter chocolate powder.

Beat the egg yolks with the sugar and spoon in the mascarpone mixing well. Separately whip the egg whites until stiff and add them to the cream, mixing gently from the bottom upwards so the whip does not collapse. Prepare the coffee, sugar lightly and as soon as it is lukewarm dip the biscuits making sure that they do not get too soggy. Cover the bottom of a cake-tin with a layer of biscuits and spread an abundant quantity of mascarpone cream over them. Start again with another layer of biscuits and so on at least three times. At the end sprinkle chocolate powder on the top layer and place in the fridge where it should stay for at least two hours before serving.

1 l milk, 4 tablespoon flour, 120 g sugar,
8 eggs, 4 tablespoons unsweetened cocoa powder,
1 lemon (zest), 500 g savoiardi (ladyfingers), 1 glass rosolio liqueur.

Zuppa inglese (trifle)

In a large, heavy-bottomed saucepan, combine the egg yolks, sugar, flour and lemon zest and whip with a whisk until the mixture is pale yellow. Pour the warm milk into the mixture and bring to the boil over low heat, stirring constantly for about 6 minutes. Remove from heat and keep stirring until the cream cools, then transfer half of the cream to a pan and stir the cocoa powder into it, making sure it has completely dissolved into the mixture. Cook for a further minute, stirring constantly. Once the creams have cooled, place a layer of ladyfingers in a large casserole (or a cake-tin), sprinkle with *rosolio* and cover with a layer of cream, followed by a layer of ladyfingers sprinkled with *rosolio*, followed by a layer of the cocoa cream, repeating this procedure until all ingredients are used up. You can garnish the *zuppa inglese* with biscuits sprinkled with liqueur. Let sit for an hour and serve.

This trifle is called "Inglese" - English because it was the favorite dessert for English people who lived in Tuscany

Pasqualina (Easter) pie

For the pastry: 750 g extra-fine flour,
50 mil extra-virgin olive oil, salt.
For the filling: 700 g Swiss chards leaves (or spinach leaves),
1 onion, fresh marjoram, 700 g ricotta cheese, 9 eggs,
100 g grated Parmesan, 1 tablespoon flour, 50 g butter,
extra-virgin olive oil, ground nutmeg (optional), salt, pepper.

Make a well with the flour, add a pinch of salt, pour the oil and enough lukewarm water to obtain a smooth, elastic dough. Divide the dough in 16 parts - 15 will have the size of an egg and one will be slightly bigger. Cover with a damp cloth and leave to rest for an hour. Meanwhile, wash and trim the chard leaves, blanch and leave to cool, then squeeze, chop and sauté in a pan with olive oil and finely chopped onion. Season with salt and pepper, add half of the Parmesan, remove from the heat and leave to cool.

In a bowl, mix the ricotta cheese with the Parmesan, the flour, 2 tablespoons of olive oil, 3 eggs, salt, pepper, the chopped marjoram and a pinch of ground nutmeg (optional). In a small bowl, mix some melted butter with olive oil and brush a round cake-tin (18-20 cm diameter) with this mixture. Roll out the bigger piece of dough into a thin sheet and place into the cake-tin, leaving the pastry overlapping the top. Roll out seven more pieces of dough into thin sheets and place them one on top of the other, brushing them with the mixture of oil and butter. Place the filling in the centre, chard leaves first. With the back of a spoon, make six hollows in the filling, place some butter and crack one egg in each hollow. Roll out the remaining parts of dough into very thin sheets and place them on top of the filling, brushing each of them with the mixture of oil and butter. Fold the overlapping pastry and braid some pastry (about 1 cm wide) to place around the edge. Brush the top sheet and bake in a pre-heated oven (190 °C) for about 45 minutes. You may cover the cake with aluminum foil to prevent the cake from burning. Serve hot.

300 g extra-fine flour,
50 g prescinseua cheese
(or fresh crescenza cheese),
extra-virgin olive oil, salt.

Make a well with the flour, pour a tablespoon of olive oil and enough luke-warm water to obtain a soft, smooth dough. Knead it well, cover it and let it rest for one hour at room temperature.

Once the dough has rested, divide it into two parts and roll out two really thin sheets. Lay a sheet on a greased baking tray and spread it with *prescinseua* cheese, then lay the second sheet of pastry over the cheese and curl the edges, squeezing them tightly to make a seal. Prick the top sheet with a fork to allow steam to escape while it cooks. Sprinkle the focaccia with olive oil and dust it with salt. Cook in a pre-heated oven (250 °C) for about 10 minutes. When the focaccia emerges from the oven, it should be golden brown. Serve hot.

Focaccia di Recco
(fresh cheese pie)

Pesto
alla Genovese

30 'Genovese' basil leaves,
120 g grated pecorino cheese ('Fiore Sardo'if possible),
100 g grated Parmesan, 2 cloves garlic,
½ glass extra-virgin olive oil from the Riviera Ligure,
50 g pine nuts (optional: nut kernels), coarse salt.

Wash the basil leaves, leave to dry on a cloth. Place the garlic and a pinch of salt in a stone mortar and grind them with a wooden pestle, then add the basil leaves and keep grinding, gently pressing the basil leaves against the sides of the mortar with the pestle, without pounding, until you obtain a smooth, creamy sauce. When you notice a bright green liquid oozing out from the ground basil leaves you can add the pine nuts, whose delicate flavour will balance the strong flavour of the garlic. Add the grated cheese and gently drizzle in the olive oil. Pesto goes perfectly with all kinds of pasta, especially *trofie*, *trofiette*, *trenette*, linguine, gnocchi and lasagne.

If you don't have a mortar, you can use a food processor, blender or chopper, possibly with plastic blades: place the basil leaves in the jar and blend it for a couple of seconds. Then add the other ingredients (except for the olive oil) and blend for another few seconds; stream the olive oil and blend until all the ingredients are finely chopped.

Trenette with Genovese pesto sauce

400 g trenette, 4 potatoes, 200 g fresh thin string beans, 1 knob of butter, salt.
For the Genovese pesto: see recipe on previous page.

Prepare a large quantity of Genovese pesto sauce. Peel the potatoes, chop them into large slices and stew them together with the string beans previously rinsed, trimmed and cut into shorter lengths if necessary. Halfway through the cooking, add the *trenette* and drain them when al dente, together with the potato slices and the string beans. Put aside some of the cooking water. Place the butter in the serving dish, add the Genovese pesto sauce, dilute with a couple of tablespoons of cooking water and pour the *trenette*, the potatoes and the string beans. Mix well and serve.

Trofie with Genovese pesto

300 extra-fine flour, 2 potatoes, 150 g green beans, 1 knob butter, salt.
For the Genovese pesto: see recipe on previous page.

Prepare the pesto following the recipe on p. ??? Make a well with the flour, add a pinch of salt and enough lukewarm water to obtain a smooth, elastic dough. Knead well, then break off pieces about the size of a hazelnut, roll them into thin sausages about 4-5 cm long. With well-floured hands, twist them into corkscrew shape. Leave the *trofie* to rest on a clean cloth for about 1 hour. Once the pasta has rested, chop the potatoes and the green beans into small cubes. Bring to the boil a large pot full of salted water, gently lower in the potatoes and cook for 10 minutes. Add the green beans, cook for 10 minutes and add the *trofie* Drain both the pasta and the vegetables after 10 minutes, while *trofie* are still al dente. Dilute the pesto sauce with a tablespoon or two of the cooking water and dress the pasta with the sauce. Mix well, sprinkled with grated cheese and serve.

Anchovies al verde

(anchovies with parsley pesto)

20 salt-packed anchovies, 2 oil-packed anchovy fillets,
1 boiled egg, 1 bunch stemmed Italian parsley, 1 stale bread
roll, ½ glass vinegar, 1 glass extra-virgin olive oil, salt, pepper.

De-salt the anchovies with cold running water, pat dry, debone them and then lay them on a serving dish. Combine the chopped parsley, the boiled egg, the anchovy fillets, the stale bread, previously soaked in vinegar - make sure you squeeze out excess vinegar before using it. Season with salt and pepper, mix well and drizzle with olive oil. Use this sauce to season the anchovies. Leave to sit for a few hours before serving.
Alternatively, you can cook the anchovies following this easy recipe: in a saucepan, sauté some crushed garlic and chopped parsley. Rinse and dry the anchovies, add them to the garlic and simmer for a few minutes. Turn them over, add chopped capers, some olives (Taggiasca variety) and white wine. Simmer until reduced and serve hot.

"al verde" means
"in green" as they
are covered by a green sauce.

1 kg octopus, 700 g potatoes,
1 clove garlic, 1 bunch parsley,
100 g black olives, pitted,
1 lemon, extra-virgin olive oil,
salt, pepper.

Octopus and potatoes salad

(from Tellaro, near La Spezia)

Bring to a boil a large pot of salted water and cook the octopus for about 10 minutes. Wash and peel the potatoes, add to the pot and cook for a further 35 minutes. Drain and chop both the potatoes and the octopus, transfer to a serving bowl and season with chopped garlic, parsley and olives. Drizzle with olive oil (from Tellaro, if possible), season with salt, freshly ground pepper and the juice of a lemon. Mix well and serve.

Sassello-style

AMARETTI

(macaroons)

300 sugar, 250 g sweet almonds,
50 g bitter almonds
(or armelline, apricot seeds),
4 eggs, butter.

Blanch and peel the almonds, dry in a pre-heated oven (150 °C) for 10 minutes, then grind in a mortar adding the sugar. If you prefer, you may also use a blender.

Whisk the egg whites to stiff peaks. Gently fold the sugar and almonds into the egg whites. Place small quantities of the mixture onto a non-stick baking sheet or in a greased baking tray. Bake in a pre-heated oven (160 °C) for about 20 minutes, until the *amaretti* are golden brown. Leave to cool on the baking tray.

500 g extra-fine flour, 150 g sugar, 50 g butter,
20 g fresh yeast, 2 eggs, 1 glass milk,
50 g raisins, 2 teaspoon aniseed,
salt, icing sugar (optional).

Liguria

Buccellato

(literally, 'shot through with holes', or 'nibbled')

Soak the raisins in a bowl of lukewarm water. Sieve the flour and make a well on a work surface, add the sugar, the softened butter, an egg, the yeast - previously dissolved in a little lukewarm water - the milk and a pinch of salt. Knead well, until you have a soft, smooth dough. Drain the raisins, squeeze excess water and add to the dough. Add the aniseed, then cover the dough and leave to raise for two hours at room temperature. Once the dough has risen, knead again and place in a greased ring-shaped cake-tin. Make little cuts in the dough, cover and leave to rise for an hour.

Before baking in the oven (pre-heated, 180 °C), brush the surface of the *bucellato* with beaten egg. Bake for about one hour and serve warm, sprinkled with icing sugar.

You can also add grated lemon zest, lemon extract or orange flower water.

Cheeses

Grana

Gorgonzola

Mozzarella

Ricotta

Emmental

Pecorino

Scamorza
affumicata

LATTE

Vitello tonnato

(braised veal with tuna mayonnaise)

500 g veal round, 200 oil-packed tuna, 4 hard-boiled eggs,
4 oil-packed fillets anchovy, 1 stick celery,
1 carrot, 1 onion, 1 bunch parsley, 1 sprig rosemary,
1 tablespoon capers, 1 lemon, 4 tablespoons mayonnaise,
½ l dry white wine, extra-virgin olive oil, salt, pepper.

In a large casserole, combine the veal, the chopped vegetables and four tablespoons of olive oil. Brown for about 10 minutes, turning the meat over in order to obtain an even, golden brown crust. Season with salt and pepper, pour in two glasses of wine and simmer for about one hour over low heat. Make sure the meat remains tender and juicy, adding more wine if necessary. Once the meat is done, remove the casserole from heat.
In a blender (or food processor), blend to a very smooth texture the eggs with the tuna fish, capers, anchovies, parsley, two tablespoons of olive oil, the juice of a lemon and a couple of tablespoons of cooking juices. If you prefer, you can add also the vegetables cooked with the meat; alternatively you can add the chopped tuna after blending the rest of the ingredients. You may also add a few tablespoons of mayonnaise, to get a smoother texture. Slice the cooled veal as thinly as you can and arrange on a serving dish. Spread the veal slices with the tuna sauce, garnish with capers and with the remaining egg cut into slices.

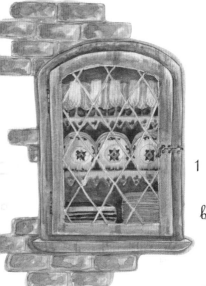

400 g rice, 2 fresh tomatoes,
peeled and seeded, 2 onions,
1 sprig rosemary,
1 tablespoon tomato pulp,
1 glass Dolcetto wine, meat stock,
400 veal marrow,
butter, pepper, grated Parmesan,
freshly sliced white truffle.

Risotto with veal marrow

In a large casserole, melt the veal marrow with a knob of butter, then add the chopped onion and some rosemary needles. As soon as the onion turns translucent, add the chopped tomatoes and the tomato pulp, season with salt and pepper and simmer for a few minutes. Add the rice, stir for a few minutes and when it has absorbed all the sauce pour the wine and simmer until reduced.

Add the hot stock gradually, stirring frequently. When the rice is al dente, remove from heat and add a few knobs of butter and some grated Parmesan. Leave to sit for a few minutes, sprinkle with freshly sliced white truffle and serve.

Agnolotti "del plin"
('plinch' agnolotti)

"plin" means a "pinch" because you pinch with thumb and forefinger to seal the little pasta packets.

For the pastry: 500 g whole-wheat flour, 6 eggs. For the filling: 300 g ground veal (rump), 300 g pork loin, 300 g escarole or endive, 2 eggs, ½ onion, 1 sprig rosemary, leaves only, 1 clove garlic, 50 g grated Parmesan, ground nutmeg, dry white wine, hot meat stock, extra-virgin olive oil, salt, pepper.

Prepare the filling: brown the meats in two separate casseroles, with some chopped onion, garlic, rosemary, salt and pepper. Pour the wine and simmer until reduced. Gradually add hot meat stock and cook for about one hour. Remove from heat, leave to cool and chop the meat finely. Pass the cooking juices through a sieve and put aside for dressing the *agnolotti*. Boil the escarole (or the endive), squeeze out excess water and sauté in a saucepan with olive oil, 2 cloves of garlic, salt and pepper. Chop it finely and mix it with the minced meat, and then add the minced meat, the eggs and the grated parmesan. Season with salt and pepper, sprinkle with ground nutmeg and mix well. If necessary, you may add another egg. Cover and leave to sit for an hour. Prepare the dough: make a well with the flour and crack in the eggs. Knead thoroughly until you have a smooth, elastic dough; if necessary, add some water or some flour, depending on the consistency of the dough. Leave to rest for 15 minutes, then divide in small portions and roll them out into thin sheets. Cut out strip 5 cm x 10 cm. Place a little heap of filling on each rectangle, fold it over to shape the *agnolotti* and pinch the edges to seal. Run a crimped pastry wheel along the bottom edge of the folded-over dough. Don't cut too close to the filling or you'll risk to break the seal. Leave to rest for a couple of hours on a floured surface, then cook in plenty of boiling salted water. Drain when al dente, dress with the sieved cooking juices and serve hot.

1 kg extra-fine flour, 10 eggs,
1 tablespoon extra-virgin olive oil, salt.

Make a well on the floured work board, crack in 2 whole eggs and 8 egg yolks, add a pinch of salt and knead well until you have a smooth, elastic dough. Cover the dough with a cloth and leave to rest for about 30 minutes (traditionally, the dough is wrapped in a damp cloth and allowed to rest for over two hours), then knead again and roll the dough out to a very thin sheet. Dust with flour, roll up the pastry sheet and cut into really thin slices (no more than 2 mm wide), using a sharp knife. Separate the *tajarin* lifting them and then dropping them on the work board, sprinkle with corn flour or durum wheat flour and leave to dry well before cooking.

TAJARIN

(tagliolini)

Fritto misto, Piedmont style
(fried meat and vegetables)

200 calf brain and bone marrow, 200 g calf sweetbread, 200 g
calf lung, 200 g sausage, 6 lamb chops, 6 slices veal liver,
6 batsoà (fried pig trotters), ¼ cauliflower, 1 courgette,
1 artichoke, 1 fennel, 100 g porcini mushroom, 1 aubergine,
2 apples, 2 soft amaretti biscuits, marsala wine, milk, 5 eggs,
all-purpose flour, dry breadcrumbs, extra-virgin olive oil, salt.
For the sweet semolina: 200 g durum wheat semolina,
150 g sugar, ½ l milk, 2-3 slices of lemon peel.

Fritto misto (deep-fried assorted meat, combined with deep-fried semolina
and macaroons) is a traditional recipe from Piedmont. It is quite a complex
dish and takes some time, and you'll have to pay special attention to the
timing, as both meat and semolina are deep-fried and must be served
together. On the other hand, it tastes fantastic! Prepare the sweet semolina:
in a saucepan, heat some milk with sugar and lemon peels. When it's just
about to boil, lower the heat and add the semolina, stirring constantly. Cook
for 20 minutes over low heat, then pour the semolina in a rectangular cake-
tin and leave to cool. You'll have to cut it into rhombuses of about 4 cm x
4 cm, so be careful about its thickness (the cream must be 1,5-2 cm thick).
Prepare the batsoà, then prepare the meat. Wash in running water veal
brains, sweetbreads, liver and lungs, then blanch in boiling water and leave
to dry on a cloth. Cut all the meat into thin slices, chop the sausages and
beat the lamb chops. Clean and trim the vegetables; cut the artichoke and
the fennel into slices, chop the courgette, the aubergine and the cauliflower.
Slice the porcini mushrooms only if they are quite big. Peel and core the
apples, cut them into rings. Prepare the macaroons just before frying all the
ingredients (remember that you have to fry before serving the dish). Dip the
amaretti biscuits first into the Marsala wine, then into the flour, then into the
beaten egg and at last into the dry breadcrumbs. Put the macaroons aside.
Dip the semolina rhombuses into the flour, then into the beaten egg and
at last into the dry breadcrumbs. Coat all the ingredients making the same
steps you've just followed for macaroons and semolina. You may prepare a
fluid and smooth batter with egg, flour and milk for the apples. Fry all the
ingredients in hot olive oil. Drain, lay on absorbent paper, sprinkle with salt
and serve immediately.

Finanziera

For 10-12 people
20 g mincemeat (veal),
200 g veal spinal column marrow (called 'filone' in Italian),
200 veal brains, 200 g veal sweetbreads,
200 g bull testicles, 200 g veal fillet, 100 g veal liver,
100 g cock's combs, 100 g veal kidneys, 100 g chicken livers,
150 g shelled peas, 150 g porcini mushrooms in oil,
1 bunch parsley, 1 glass Barolo wine, Marsala,
vinegar, all-purpose flour, butter, salt pepper.

Finanziera is a rather complex and time-consuming recipe. In a small casserole, bring to the boil some water with vinegar, parsley and salt. Blanch one by one the sweetbreads, cock's combs, *filone* and brains, then leave to dry on a cloth. Cut the veal fillets into thin strips, form little knots and put aside. Cut into strips or chunks all the meat and dip into the flour. Brown quickly in a pan with olive oil (remember to change it frequently, to preserve the taste of the meat). Prepare little meatballs (the size of a nut) with the mincemeat, dip into the flour and put aside. In a large casserole, sauté the veal knots with some butter, then lower the heat and continue cooking. In a small saucepan, sauté the veal kidneys, then add to the veal knots, sprinkle with Barolo wine and stir well. Sauté the meatballs in the saucepan, then transfer to the casserole and pour some more Barolo wine. Follow these steps with the cock's combs, veal liver, chicken liver, sweetbreads, *filone*, bull testicles, veal brains. When all the meat has been browned, season with salt and pepper, and add the green peas and the sliced mushrooms. Stir well and leave to simmer, adding some wine if necessary. Shortly before serving, sprinkle with some vinegar and some Marsala wine. Serve hot.

Finanziera is the Italian name of a male dress, called also stiffelius or redingote.

Hazelnut cake

(crescent-shaped cookies from Monferrato region in Piemonte)

150 g Piedmont hazelnuts,
250 g extra-fine flour, 200 g sugar,
3 eggs, 150 g butter,
1 sachet baking powder, milk.

Lay the hazelnuts on a baking tray and toast in a pre-heated oven (160 °C), then grind in a mortar until you obtain a coarse mixture. Beat the egg yolks with sugar until you have a soft and spongy mixture. Beat the egg whites until stiff, then slowly fold in the flour, the egg yolks mixture, the ground hazelnuts, the baking powder and the melted butter. Mix well and add some milk if necessary.

Pour the mixture in a lined cake-tin and bake in a pre-heated oven (180 °C) for 30-40 minutes.

Blanc manger

1 l cream, 1 vanilla pod,
6 tablespoon sugar,
10 g gelatin (or fish glue),
dry cookies or wild berries.

Pour two tablespoons of sugar in a cake tin and caramelise it over low heat. Put aside to cool.

In a saucepan, combine the cream with the sugar, vanilla pod and gelatin (previously soaked in lukewarm water) Bring to the boil over low heat, stirring constantly. When the gelatin has completely melted, remove the vanilla pod and pour the cream into the cake tin. Leave to chill in the fridge for a couple of hours, and then flip it onto a serving plate, together with some dry cookies or wild berries.

Crumiri

280 g meliga
(finely ground corn meal),
200 g all-purpose flour,
280 g butter, 160 g sugar,
4 egg yolks, 1 sachet vanilla extract.

Break the butter into bits and leave at room temperature to soften. Pass the meliga and the all-purpose flour through a sieve, then make a well on the breadboard and add the sugar and vanilla extract. Incorporate the softened butter and the egg yolks, and keep kneading thoroughly until you have a soft, smooth dough. Cover with plastic wrap and leave to sit for an hour in a cool place. Put the dough in a pastry bag (choose a tip with a jagged edge) and lay on a lined baking tray little crescent-shaped cookies, about 8 cm long. Bake in a pre-heated oven for about 20 minutes, when the *crumiri* are golden brown. These delicious cookies can be successfully stored in tins or glass jars.

BONET

(Piemontese traditional sweet pudding)

200 g chestnuts from Val di Susa, ½ l milk, 6 tablespoons sugar, 4 eggs, 2 dessert spoons unsweetened cocoa powder, 1 vanilla pod, 1 glass rum, 1 handful sweet hazelnuts from Piedmont.

With a sharp knife, make a cross-cut across the skin of the chestnuts. Boil the chestnuts for about 40 minutes and peel them while they are still hot. Pass through a sieve and leave to cool. Beat the 4 egg yolks with 4 tablespoons of sugar, carefully fold in the chestnut puree, the cocoa powder and the rum. Pour the milk in a pot, add the vanilla pod and bring to a boil, then remove the vanilla pod, remove the pot from heat and leave to cool. Add the milk to the chestnuts puree and fold in the stiffly-beaten egg whites.

Pre-heat your oven to 180 °C. While it's heating, pour the remaining sugar in a mold and heat it over a flame to caramelise it; pivot the mold to coat its sides with the caramelised sugar. Fill the mold with the pudding, and bake it in the oven, in a pan of water (bain marie) for about 45 minutes. Remove the *bonet* from the oven, let it cool and unmold it onto a serving dish, and serve, garnished with whipped cream and coarsely ground hazelnuts.

Fonduta valdostana

(cheese fondue from the Val d'Aosta)

500 g fontina cheese, 1 l milk,
80 g butter, 4 eggs,
toasted bread, salt, pepper.

Dice or finely slice the *fontina* cheese and marinate it in the milk overnight. Once it has soaked, melt the butter with a little milk in a double saucepan, then add the fontina and the egg yolks, stirring carefully until the cheese is completely melted. During the cooking time, the cheese will melt, forming strings, and then thicken again. Season with salt and pepper.

When you have a smooth, dense cream, turn off the heat and serve immediately, with slices of toasted bread. You may sprinkle the *Fonduta* with freshly ground black truffle.

A recommended accompaniment to cheese fondue is Enfer d'Arvier, a wine from Val d'Aosta - garnet colored and with a characteristic velvety, slightly bitter, taste.

Bresaola, arugula and Parmesan

200 g bresaola
(air-cured beef, from the Valtellina),
thinly sliced, 100 g parmesan shavings,
2 bunches arugula (rocket salad), 1 lemon,
extra-virgin olive oil, salt, pepper.

Lay the slices of *bresaola* on a serving dish, drizzle with olive oil and season with salt, pepper and lemon juice. Arrange the Parmesan shavings and the shredded arugula over the *bresaola*, keep in the refridgerator until serving.

Mostarda di Cremona

(pickled fruit with mustard sauce)

1,5 kg fruit, not too ripe (figs, tangerines, apricots, oranges, citrons, pears, peaches, quinces, cherries), 1,5 kg sugar, 60 g powdered mustard seeds, 1 organic lemon.

Peel the citruses and divide into wedges. Wash all the fruit and pat dry, then core and quarter pears and quinces. In a large earthenware pot, pour 3 cups of water, add 500 g of sugar and the grated zest of the lemon. Melt the sugar over a high heat, stirring constantly. Add the fruit and simmer for about 30 minutes, stirring frequently. When the fruit mixture is ready, turn off the heat and let it cool. Transfer the fruit on a lined baking tray and put in a pre-heated oven at a low temperature, so that the fruit dries up. In the meantime, heat 2-3 cups of water, add the remaining sugar and the mustard, beating the mixture with a whisk until you obtain a dense, clear syrup. Transfer the fruit from the baking tray to sterile jars, filling them up as much as possible. Pour the mustard syrup over the fruit, seal the jars and store them in a cool dry place for at least a month. Traditionally, *Mostarda di Cremona* goes well with roast or boiled meat, or with *cotechino*

Pizzoccheri della Valtellina

(buckwheat pasta with cheese, potatoes and greens)

For the pasta: 300 g of buckwheat flour, 100 g extra-fine flour, 1 egg yolk, salt. For the sauce: 300 Savoy cabbage, 3 potatoes, 1 onion, 1 clove of garlic, 200 g unseasoned Bitto or Valtellina Casera (alternatively, you can use Fontina or Asiago), 4 sage leaves, 4 tablespoons grated Grana Padano cheese, 100 g butter, salt, pepper.

Mix the two kinds of flour on a floured breadboard and make a mound with a well in the centre. Add the egg yolk and a pinch of salt. Add enough water to blend, and knead thoroughly until you have a firm, elastic dough. With a rolling-pin, roll out a sheet not too thin (about 3 mm thick) and cut into strip about 1 cm wide and 4-6 cm long. Leave them to dry on a flour-sprinkled cloth. Peel the onion and the garlic, cut them into thin slices, add the chopped sage and sauté for about 10 minutes in butter over medium heat. Turn off the heat and set aside to rest. Wash the Savoy cabbage, remove the core and the thick leaves on the very outside of the cabbage, and then cut it into strips. Wash and peel the potatoes, then cut them into cubes. Bring a pot of salted water to the boil, and add the savoy cabbage and the diced potatoes. After about 20 minutes add the *pizzoccheri* and cook for about 10 minutes. Drain the potatoes, the cabbage and the pasta when the latest is al dente. Transfer to a serving dish, dress with the onion and garlic sauce, add the Bitto cheese finely cubed and the grated Grana Padano. Stir, add a pinch of pepper and serve immediately.

Turtéi d' süca

(tortelli with pumpkin filling)

Tortelli are stuffed pasta. This recipe is a Medieval traditional dish of Mantua. The stuffing inside the tortelli is rather sweet.

This dish boasts noble origins and appears in a recipe of 1584, signed by Lucrezia d'Este's butler. According to tradition, the Gonzaga family considered this dish as a symbol of their Court. The recipe was enhanced with the addition of mustard, in order to emphasize the contrast between sweet and salty flavour, very popular in the Middle Ages. Pumpkin tortellini is the traditional Christmas Eve dish.

For 6 people

For the pastry: 5 eggs, 500 g durum wheat flour, 1 tablespoon extra-virgin olive oil.

For the filling: 1.5 kg pumpkin (round pumpkin, with very floury pulp), 200 g amaretti (macaroons), 200 g mustard from Mantova, 1 egg, nutmeg, grated Parmesan cheese, salt.

For the sauce: 50 g butter, 4 tablespoons grated Parmesan cheese.

Cut the pumpkin, without removing the peel and cook the pieces (preferably in the oven). Once cooled, remove the pumpkin peel and seeds, collect the pulp into a large bowl and mix with finely crushed amaretti biscuits, egg, mustard, nutmeg and lots of parmesan. The dough should be left to rest in a cool place for a couple of hours so that all the flavors blend well. In the meantime, prepare the dough: make a well with the flour, add the eggs and the oil. Knead well and roll out to a thin sheet. Cut out small squares of dough (8x4 cm), then spread a teaspoon of pumpkin mixture on each. Fold each square into two and press together the edges of the rectangles. Cook the ravioli in salted water, drain and toss in a large baking dish in layers. Each layer should be sprinkled with melted butter and grated parmesan cheese.

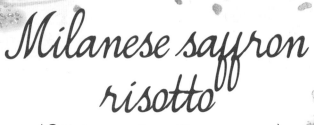

Milanese saffron risotto

(Milan-style soffron risotto)

400 g Vialone nano rice, 20 g beef marrow,
½ onion, ½ glass dry white wine,
1,5 l meat stock (or vegetable stock),
1 sachet saffron, 60 g butter, 100 g grated Parmesan,
4 tablespoons extra-virgin olive oil, salt.

In a large saucepan, sauté the beef bone marrow and the finely sliced onion with some olive oil, over an extremely low flame. As soon as the onion becomes translucent, add the rice stirring constantly lest it stick and burn. Season with salt, pour the wine and simmer until reduced. Stir in the hot stock a ladle at a time, and about five minutes before the rice is done, stir in the saffron, diluted in a couple of tablespoons of hot stock. Turn off the flame, add the butter and the grated Parmesan, stir well and let the risotto sit covered for a couple of minutes before serving.

Risotto alla pilòta

"The pilota" was the person who worked the pila, or ricemill, because they turned the "pile", a large stone mortar which was used to separate the rice from the husk

(rice with minced salalmi)

360 Vialone nano rice, 300 g fresh minced salami from Mantova (or any other low-fat salamella), 40 g butter, 4 tablespoons extra-virgin olive oil, 4 tablespoons grated Parmesan, salt.

In a large double-bottom saucepan, bring bring a litre of water with a pinch of salt to the boil and a pinch of salt. Remember to stick to the given ratio of rice to water, in order to have all the water absorbed by the rice. According to locals, you should use 250 ml of cold water to 250 g of rice. Pour the rice into the boiling water to form a pyramid, with its top just below the surface of the water. Do not stir but lightly shake the saucepan to collapse the pyramid. Cook over high heat (don't cover the pan) for 10-12 minutes - not counting the time it takes to bring the water back to a boil, of course! When all the water has been absorbed, remove the saucepan from heat and stir the rice. Cover with a clean cotton cloth, then cover with a lid and place a heavy object on top of it, in order to close the saucepan hermetically. Leave to stand for a further 10 minutes. When you remove the lid and the cloth, the rice should be firm and dry. Meanwhile, peel the *salamella*, mince it and sauté over low heat in a small saucepan with olive oil and butter. Stir well, then add the meat and its cooking juices to the cooked rice. Add half of the Parmesan and stir to combine. Serve immediately, sprinkled with the rest of the Parmesan.

12 courgette flowers,
150 g Emmental or ricotta cheese, 2 courgettes,
2 tablespoons grated Parmesan, 1 clove garlic,
1 bunch parsley, 4 leaves basil, 4 tablespoons
extra-virgin olive oil, peanut oil for frying, salt.
For the batter: 150 g all-purpose flour, 1 sachet baking
powder, 1 egg, 1 glass milk, 1 pinch salt.

Stuffed deep-fried courgette flowers

Heat the oil in a deep, heavy-based pan. Wash, trim and chop the courgettes. Sauté in a pan with olive oil and the crushed garlic, the minced parsley and a pinch of salt. Simmer for 10 minutes, then remove from heat and transfer to a bowl to cool. When the courgettes are cold, add the grated Parmesan, the shredded Emmental and the shredded basil. Mix well to combine all the ingredients. Prepare the batter: in a clean bowl, combine the milk, egg, flour, baking powder and a pinch of salt. Whisk well to form a batter, adding some water or some more flour if necessary. Wash and pat dry the courgette flowers, trim them and cut them longwise. Fill each courgette flower with a spoonful of the cheese mixture, then dip the courgette flowers into the batter and transfer to the oil to deep-fry until evenly golden brown. Remove from the oil with a slotted spoon and drain on kitchen paper. Serve hot.

Milanese veal cutlet

4 veal cutlets on the bone, 2 eggs, 100 g extra-fine flour, 100 g breadcrumbs, 100 g butter (or 6 tablespoons extra-virgin olive oil), salt.

Tenderize the veal cutlets with a meat mallet, dredge them with flour, then dip in the beaten egg and dredge in the breadcrumbs, pressing the meat between your palms to make sure the breadcrumbs stick. In the meantime, melt the butter in a skillet large enough to contain all 4 cutlets at once, and when it begins to crackle add them. Cook quickly turning once so both sides brown, remove from heat and leave to dry on absorbent paper. Alternatively, you can cook the meat with olive oil. Serve hot, drizzled with lemon juice (or, following the tradition, with the melted butter you cooked the cutlets in) and sprinkled with salt, accompanied with vegetables. For a more refined touch, you can wrap the cutlet bone with aluminum foil, so that your guests will be able to pick it clean.

Ossibuchi with peas

4 ossibuchi (sliced veal shanks), 200 g peas (fresh or frozen), 1 white onion, 1 clove garlic, 2 ripe tomatoes, 2 tablespoons all-purpose flour, 1 bunch parsley, 1 glass dry white wine, ½ organic lemon, salt, pepper.

Make cuts in several points of the membranes surrounding the ossibuchi or they will shrink, causing the ossibuchi to curl as they cook. Dredge with flour the ossibuchi, and set aside. In a large heavy-bottom pan, sauté the finely chopped onion and the crushed garlic. Add the ossibuchi and brown them on both sides, sprinkling them every now and then with the wine. Cover the pan with a lid and leave to simmer for 10 minutes. Add the peas and the tomatoes, previously peeled and chopped. Season with salt and pour ½ litre of hot water (or hot meat broth), cover with a lid and leave to cook for about 1 hour, turning the ossibuchi over half way through the cooking and adding more hot broth if necessary, to keep the ossibuchi from drying out. Once the meat is very tender, remove from heat and sprinkle with chopped parsley, grated lemon zest and freshly ground black pepper. Serve immediately.

"Ossobuco" is a bone=osso with a hole=buco

La sbrisolona
(Typical crunchy tart from mantua)

200 g extra-fine flour,
200 g finely ground corn flour,
200 g lard, 150 g sugar,
200 g ground toasted almonds,
3 eggs, grated lemon peel (1 lemon),
1 teaspoon baking powder.
For the cake-tin: butter.

Sbrisolona ('crumbly') is a typical traditional cake from Mantova. Grease and flour the cake-tin. Pass the two kinds of flour through a sieve, make a well on the breadboard and add the sugar (keep two tablespoons aside), almonds, grated lemon peel, eggs and melted lard. Work the ingredients quickly with the top of your fingers to form a crumbly mixture; don't expect it to be homogeneous. Crumble the cake mixture into the cake tin, rolling the blebs between your fingers to break them up - they'll come together again as they bake. Bake the cake in a pre-heated oven (180 °C) for 30-40 minutes.

Panettone

700 g extra-fine flour, 250 g sugar, 250 g butter, 25 g fresh yeast, 6 egg yolks, 100 g raisins, 50 g candied orange peel, 50 g candied lime peel, grated organic lemon zest (1 lemon), 1 teaspoon extra-fine flour, 1 teaspoon salt, butter for greasing the cake-tin.

Prepare the first rising: dissolve the yeast in a little lukewarm water, add 100 g flour and form a rather firm dough. Transfer it to a bowl, cover with a damp cloth (dampened in warm water and then squeezed) and leave to rise in a warm place. Half an hour later, add 300 g flour and some lukewarm water and knead thoroughly to form a consistent dough. Shape into a ball, place in a larger bowl, cover with a cloth and leave to rise in a warm place for a couple of hours. Once the dough has doubled in size, add the remaining flour, the butter melted in a bain marie (keep aside 50 g for later), the egg yolk (previously beaten with the sugar), the grated lemon zest and a pinch of salt. Knead thoroughly for about 10 minutes, until you have a smooth, soft dough. Add the crumbled candied orange and lime peels. Soak the raisins in lukewarm water, drain them, squeeze excess water, dust with flour and add them to the dough. Line the *panettone* cake-tin (round and high-sided) with greased baking paper, and set the dough inside. The dough should fill only half the cake-tin. Cover with a cloth and leave to rise in a warm place for a couple of hours. Once the dough has doubled its size, cut a cross-cut into the top of the *panettone*, put the remaining butter all over (divided into small bits) and put in a pre-heated oven (180 °C) for about 40 minutes. Half-way through the baking, lower the temperature of the oven to 160°. Make sure you never open the oven while the *panettone* is cooking. Bake the *panettone* until a skewer inserted into the middle comes out dry. When the *panettone* is ready, turn off the oven and open its door, leaving the *panettone* to cool in the oven. After a few minutes, take it out of the oven and leave to cool on a rack. Take it off the mould only when it's completely cold.

Torta delle rose
(rose cake)

400 g extra-fine flour, 180 sugar,
100 g butter, 100 g fresh yeast, 3 dl milk,
3 tablespoons corn oil, 3 egg yolks, 2 egg whites,
1 lemon, icing sugar, salt.
Butter and flour to grease the cake-tin.

Warm the milk and dissolve the fresh yeast in it, add a pinch of salt, 50 g sugar, the oil, butter, grated zest, flour, 3 egg yolks and 2 egg whites. Knead thoroughly until you have a soft, smooth dough. Shape in form of a ball, place in a bowl and cover with a cloth. Pre-heat the oven, and when it's warm turn off the heat and leave the dough to rise in the oven for an hour, together with a bowl of water. While the dough is rising, leave the butter to soften at room temperature. Add the remaining sugar and whisk with a fork until you have a soft, creamy mixture. Once the dough has risen, knead it again and roll out to a sheet I cm thick. Spread the creamy mixture on the pastry sheet and roll it up in a cylinder. Cut the roll into slices about 5 cm wide, pressing together the lower rim to seal it, so that the filling doesn't ooze out. Butter and flour a cake-tin, lay the rolls of pastry upright, leaving I cm between the 'rosebuds'. Place the cake-tin in the warm oven (heat turned off!) with a bowl of water and leave to rise for about I ½ hours. Wait for the "rosebuds" to stick together: this means they have completed their leavening. Remove the bowl of water, and turn the oven on (180 °C). Bake the cake for about 30 minutes. When the 'rosebuds' are golden brown, remove from the oven and sprinkle with icing sugar.

1 pike of 600 g, 20 g anchovies, capers 20 g,
1 clove garlic, 1 bunch parsley, ground cinnamon,
6 tablespoons extra-virgin olive oil.
For the court-bouillon with vinegar: 1.5 l vinegar,
200 g onions, 150 g carrots, 5-6 parsley stems, 2-3 bay
leaves, 5-6 black pepper grains.
To complete: 8 slices of polenta.

Pike with sauce and polenta

For this recipe you'll need two litres of court bouillon with vinegar. Peel the onions, carrots and slice them coarsely. Put the vegetables in the fish-kettle with vinegar, laurel, parsley, pepper and pour at least two litres of water. Simmer for half an hour, then strain the liquid with a fine-mesh strainer. Clean, gut and scale the pike, wash it and then dip it in the court-bouillon. Cook over medium heat for about half an hour. Make sure not to bring the court-bouillon to the boil. Once cooked, drain the fish, let it cool at room temperature and remove bones and skin. Pick up the meat in a baking dish, sprinkle with cinnamon and let sit for about ten minutes. In a saucepan, heat the oil, sauté the garlic - remove it when golden brown - add the chopped anchovies, some whole capers and a mixture of chopped parsley and capers.

Stir gently keeping the flame very low, then sprinkle the pike with the sauce. Put to rest in the fridge for half a day, then serve with slices of grilled *polenta*

The fabulous story of the three sisters and their special *polenta*

Once upon a time, there were three sisters: Albina, Gisella and Linda. They lived in a small village in Northern Italy; at a very young age they learned to prepare a delicious *polenta*, which soon became famous all over the region. They led a very simple life, and maybe this was the secret of their superb *polenta*. Here comes their story, enjoy it! Albina was born in 1891: she started stirring *polenta* when she was only twelve, and cooked a *polenta* a day until she was eighty-one. If you think about it, she must have been stirring over twenty-five thousands cauldrons of *polenta*! Her sister Gisella, nine years younger than her, helped pouring the corn flour in the boiling water and cooked nearly twenty-two thousand cauldrons of *polenta*. Linda, the youngest, helped her two sisters preparing nearly nineteen thousand cauldrons of *polenta*. What a family! During the long winter evenings, Gisella would light a fire in the fireplace and would put a large pot of water to boil. When the water started boiling, she added some salt - a bit at a time, so it would dissolve evenly in the boiling water. She would then pass the corn flour through a sieve and pour it slowly into the boiling water, while Albina would keep stirring clockwise. When the *polenta* was quite dense and lots of air bubbles started coming to the surface, Albina and Gisella would slow down their pace to allow the golden mixture to cook evenly. The two sisters would keep stirring from time to time until the *polenta* reached the right texture: the whole process could take between thirty and forty minutes. In the meantime, Gisella would stoke the fire with the "casteloni" and would then prepare the "caza", a jar of water to sprinkle on the sides of the cauldron, in order to soften the scorched bits of *polenta* ready to be scraped off from the sides of the cauldron and eaten.

A delicious smell would soon announce that the *polenta* was ready: Albina, with a wet spatula, would then clean the *"mescola*, a long, wooden spoon used to stir *polenta* With the same spatula, she would lightly press the edges of the *polenta*: she knew that if the creamy golden mixture did not stick to the sides of the cauldron, their delicious *polenta* was ready to be poured il on the panara, a special round wooden breadboard with a diameter of about 55 cm. Linda would then bring a cold plate: she would hold it over the *polenta*, about ten centimeters away, to get it wet with condensation. Then she would press the plate on the *polenta*: the wet plate worked as a sort of mold, so the *polenta* could be adjusted to the *panara* in less than a minute, ready to be cut with a piece of kitchen twine. The flour came from our corn: the cobs were shelled by hand and then ground in water mills next to the river Adige. Freshly ground corn flour doesn't make *panarono* (lumps) when its poured into hot boiling water. Polenta at room temperature goes very well with raw *treolòti*.

"Polenta apena Brustolà la va con tuto!" (Slighty toasted polenta goes with everything!) *"Na scudela de late caldo, zucaro e polenta brustolà"* (a bowl of hot milk, sugar and polenta) is a delicious breakfast, and before bed it will help you sleep.

Polenta
300 g of corn flour, salt.

In a large copper pot, bring to the boil a litre of water. Add a pinch of salt and stir in the corn flour, stirring vigorously with a whisk to avoid the formation of lumps. Cook for half an hour, stirring from time to time. When it's cooked, pour the *polenta* on the traditional wooden cutting board and let cool down a bit before cutting into slices. Serve hot. If you want to prepare country-style polenta, rather compact, you should use coarsely ground corn - the ratio is 350 grams per litre of water. If you prefer your *polenta* to be rather soft, use finely ground corn, and lower the dose of corn to 250 grams per litre of water.

Pasta e fagioli

130 g of noodles, 500 g of fresh shelled beans, 100 g of bacon or lard, 2 potatoes, 1 onion, butter, vegetable broth (or low fat meat broth), extra-virgin olive oil, salt and pepper.

Simmer the beans in plenty of lightly salted water for 10 minutes, then drain and transfer them to a saucepan with plenty of hot vegetable stock and a couple of peeled potatoes cut into chunks. In a pan, fry the chopped bacon (or lard) in oil and butter. After a few minutes, add the chopped onion and turn off the heat as soon as it becomes translucent and soft. Drain the potatoes and beans and mash a part (if possible, remove the skins of the vegetables), then put them back to the saucepan in their broth, adding the fried bacon and onion. Season with salt and pepper, bring the soup to a boil, then add the noodles. Pasta e fagioli is excellent hot or warm. If you use dried beans leave them to soak in cold water for at least 12 hours before cooking.

Bon brusà with lard

100 g flour, 300 g bacon, rosemary, 1 clove garlic, salt.

On a cutting board, prepare a bacon, rosemary and garlic mince. When the mince is creamy add the flour. Toast the mixture in a frying pan, stirring constantly. Bon brusà will be ready when the creamy mixture becomes brown. This mixture is the true secret to the "pasta and beans soupe" from Verona, try it!

Brò brusà with oil

100 g flour, 1 cup extra virgin olive oil, salt and pepper.

Heat in a pan the oil, add the flour and stir well until it is golden brown. Dilute with warm salted water, beating with a whisk until you have a dense broth. Season with salt and pepper and serve.

400 g pappardelle,
300 g chicken livers, 50 g butter,
1.5 2 l good chicken or turkey broth,
grated Parmesan, salt.

Pappardelle
with chicken livers

Prepare the sauce: clean the chicken livers, cut them into small pieces and brown them in the butter, then add a pinch of salt and simmer for a few minutes over low heat. In a saucepan, bring the broth to a boil and pour the *pappardelle* Drain the pasta when al dente, transfer to the pan with the sauce, sprinkle with grated Parmesan and serve

Valeggio-style *tortellini*

For the pasta: 400 g extra-fine flour, 3 eggs, salt.
For the filling: 100 g ground pork, 100 g ground beef,
100 g minced chicken meat, 50 g minced Parma ham,
1 egg yolk, 50 g grated Parmesan cheese,
50 g breadcrumbs, 1 onion, 1 sprig of rosemary,
1 glass dry white wine, 4 tablespoons extra-virgin
olive oil, 1 pinch grated nutmeg, salt and pepper.
For the sauce: 50 g butter,
4 tablespoons grated Parmesan cheese, 2 sage leaves.

In a pan, sauté the chopped onion, add the chopped meat and simmer for a few minutes. Pour the wine and the chopped rosemary needles, season with salt and pepper. Stir, lower the heat, cover the pan and cook until the meat is tender. If the meat sauce gets too dry, add a little warm water - once the meat is cooked, the extra water should have been completely absorbed. Leave to cool and then place in a blender, add the ham, Parmesan, egg yolk, nutmeg, breadcrumbs and mix well. Form a ball and put to rest in a bowl for half an hour. Prepare the dough: make a well with the flour, add the eggs, a pinch of salt and as much water as needed (about half a glass) to obtain a smooth and firm dough. Roll it out to a thin sheet - try not to sprinkle the dough with flour while rolling it out, otherwise it'll be really difficult to seal the tortellini. Cut the pasta sheet into squares of about 4-5 cm with a pastry wheel. Place a coffee spoon of filling in the center of each square, fold the dough over itself in a triangle, lining up the edges and pressing to seal them. Then fold the two opposite corners of the triangle, overlap them and pinch them together. You will get small rings of stuffed pasta. Leave the tortellini on a tablecloth to dry. In a pan, sauté the chopped sage leaves with the butter. Boil the tortellini in salted water for a few minutes: when they come to the surface, drain them with a slotted spoon and pour in individual dishes. Season with the melted butter, sprinkle with Parmesan cheese and serve.

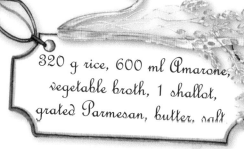

320 g rice, 600 ml Amarone, vegetable broth, 1 shallot, grated Parmesan, butter, salt

Peel the shallots, slice them finely and sauté them over low heat with the butter. When the shallots are translucent, add the rice and toast it until it is translucent as well. Pour a glass of wine and simmer until reduced. Cook the *risotto*, alternating ladles of hot broth and wine glasses.

When the rice is al dente, season with salt and stir in a knob of butter and some grated Parmesan. Let the risotto rest for a few minutes before serving.

Risotto with Amarone
della Valpolicella wine

(intensely flavored red wine made from dried-passito grapes in Valpolicella, near Verona)

Risotto with asparagus

360 g rice, 1 bunch of fresh asparagus
(300 g of frozen asparagus),
1 onion, 1 sprig of parsley,
200 g of creamy cheese (robiola or other),
100 g grated Parmesan, 50 g butter, 4 tablespoons
extra-virgin olive oil, salt.

Boil the asparagus for 10 minutes in two litres of hot salted water. Drain them and put the cooking water aside. Cut off the tops of the asparagus and chop them, then blend the stems with a little of their own cooking water. In a pan, sauté the onion (previously finely chopped), add the rice and let it toast slightly. Gradually pour the hot cooking water of the asparagus, stirring constantly. Leave the pan uncovered and cook the rice for about 15-18 minutes, until al dente. About 5 minutes before turning off the heat, add the asparagus tips and also the pureed stems. Stir well, turn off the heat, add the chopped parsley, the soft cheese, butter and parmesan.
Mix thoroughly, cover and let rest for a few minutes. Serve hot.

Risotto al nero di seppia

(black risotto with cuttlefish ink)

600 g cuttlefish, with its ink sack,
300 g of rice Vialone, 1 l fish stock,
1 small onion, 1 clove of garlic, 30 g butter,
1 cup of extra-virgin olive oil,
1 glass of wine dry white wine, salt and pepper.

Skin and ink the cuttlefish, removing the unnecessary parts, i.e. the bone, eyes, mouth and stomach; set aside the ink sacks. Wash the cuttlefish well and cut into thin slices. Finely chop the onion and sauté with a clove of garlic in a saucepan with a little olive oil. When the garlic begins to brown, remove it and add the cuttlefish. Season with salt and pepper and cook for a few minutes, stirring, then add the wine and simmer until reduced. Dilute the black ink in a little water, pour it into the saucepan and cook for about twenty minutes. Then pour the rice; as soon as the rice absorbs the color from the ink, stir in hot fish stock, a ladle full at a time until the rice reaches the al dente stage. Season with butter, chopped parsley and mix well. Wait a few minutes before serving, accompanying with Pinot Grigio Lison-Pramaggiore wine.

Wash the potatoes and cook them - un-peeled - in plenty of salted water until they are soft but still firm. Peel them and mash them while they're still hot (a potato ricer works very well here). Season the potatoes with a pinch of salt and slowly knead in the egg and enough flour to obtain a fairly firm, smooth, non-sticky dough - exactly how much flour will depend upon how moist the potatoes are. Roll the dough out into snakes about as thick as your finger, cut the snakes into one-inch pieces, and gently score the pieces crosswise with a fork. As an alternative to scoring with a fork, you can gently press them against the inside of a curved cheese grater. Then put the dumplings on a tablecloth, leaving enough space between them. Bring to the boil a large pan of salted water and gently pour the *gnocchi*, collecting them with a slotted spoon as soon as they rise to the surface. Serve hot in a bowl, ready to be seasoned with meat sauce, tomato sauce, or melted butter and sage.

Potato gnocchi

6 potatoes (medium size), 200 g flour, 1 egg, salt.

Pearà sauce

"Pearà" means peppered

1 l of meat stock (beef and chicken),
500 g stale bread crumbs,
100 g beef marrow, 50 g butter,
80 g grated Parmesan, 4 tablespoons extra-virgin olive oil,
salt, 2 teaspoons freshly ground black pepper.

Place a medium size earthenware pot - protected by a heat-diffuser plate - over very low heat, and melt the butter and the beef marrow stirring with a wooden spoon. Pour the boiling broth and slowly stir in the bread crumbs and the freshly ground pepper, stirring until the mixture is smooth. Drizzle with olive oil without stirring, covering the entire surface of the sauce: the oil will work as a lid. Bring to a boil, lower the heat, and simmer for about 2 hours in the uncovered pan. When the pearà sauce is cooked, stir in the grated Parmesan cheese and season with salt and pepper. Pearà should be thick and creamy. Serve hot. Traditionally, pearà sauce accompanies bollito misto (boiled beef and chicken meat).

Bollito misto

(boiled mixed beef and chicken meat)

1 free-range chicken,
1 kg young beef (preferably top round),
1 cotechino (spiced pork sausage), 500 g calf's brains,
a pickled tongue, 1 carrot, 1 onion, 1 celery stick, salt.

Clean and wash the chicken and the beef. Boil in a pot full of salted water with the carrot, onion and celery, previously cleaned and coarsely cut. Cook for about two and a half hours, skimming every so often.

Meanwhile cook separately the *cotechino*, the calf's brains and the pickled tongue; to make sure the skin of the *cotechino* doesn't burst, pinch it crossing two wooden skewers next to each end of the sausage; as for the pickled tongue, make sure you replace the cooking water at least once. Even the calf's brains should be boiled separately. Once it is cooked, slice the meat and serve hot. Boiled meat goes well with *pearà*, but also with *crèn* (horseradish sauce), a sauce prepared by grating the roots of *Armoracia rusticana*, seasoned with vinegar and stored in oil in glass jars.

Fegato alla veneziana

(Venetian style liver)

600 g calf's liver cut into thin
slices, 1 large white onion,
1 sprig of parsley, flour,
30 g butter, 4 tablespoons
of extra virgin olive oil,
1 tablespoon white wine vinegar,
salt, pepper.

Peel and slice the onion into rings. In a pan, sauté the onion rings with four tablespoons of oil and two tablespoons of water over low heat for about 20 minutes. When the onion is cooked, remove from the pan with a slotted spoon. Turn up the heat, add the butter and the liver, previously lightly floured. Cook for a maximum of 5 minutes - liver tends to harden quickly -, stirring constantly. Add the sautéed onion, sprinkle with vinegar, salt and pepper, flavour with chopped parsley, stir and cook for a further minute. Serve immediately, with the traditional Venetian white polenta.

Baccalà

alla vicentina

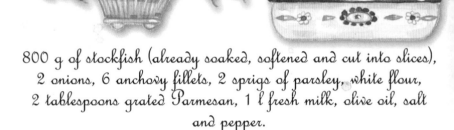

800 g of stockfish (already soaked, softened and cut into slices),
2 onions, 6 anchovy fillets, 2 sprigs of parsley, white flour,
2 tablespoons grated Parmesan, 1 l fresh milk, olive oil, salt
and pepper.

Skin and bone the sliced stockfish, cut it into small pieces and cover them in flour. Slice the onions and sauté them in a pan with four tablespoons of olive oil, then add the anchovies and mince them with a fork. In a double-bottom steel pan (make sure you choose the right size for the pan, otherwise you'll need more milk and oil), spread a few tablespoons of sautéed onion, lay the stockfish, and cover with a layer of sautéed onions. Continue alternating layers of onions and stockfish until all the ingredients are used. Pour all of the milk very slowly, sprinkle with Parmesan cheese, season with salt and pepper and drizzle with oil. The stockfish must be completely covered by the mixture of milk and oil. Cook the fish over extremely low heat ("*pipare*", as they say in Veneto) for about 2 hours, occasionally moving it gently with a spatula (never turn the fish upside down, or it will break) or shaking the pot by the handles. Some people, though, prefer the stockfish to be crumbled. Sprinkle with freshly chopped parsley and serve with hot white or yellow *polenta*. According to connoisseurs, stockfish is better after 12-24 hours. Its sauce is also indicated for dressing pasta or gnocchi.

Sarde in saòr

(Venetian-style sweet and sour sardines)

kg of sardines, 1 kg of white onions,
3 dl white wine vinegar, peanut oil or sunflower oil,
flour, salt, 50 g of pine nuts
and 100 g of raisins soaked (optional).

Many years ago, Venetian fishermen worked out a tasty way to preserve freshly caught fish for a long time. The trick is to fry the fish and then leave to marinate in a mixture of onions and vinegar. Clean the sardines by removing the head and entrails, wash gently under running cold water and leave to drain in a colander for half an hour before pat drying with paper towels. Flour in a sieve in order to remove excess flour, then fry them in hot oil for 3 minutes. Drain with a strainer and place them on paper towels. Season with salt and put aside. In a pan, sauté the peeled and thinly sliced onions, add half a glass of water and simmer over low heat until the onions become translucent. Season with salt, pour the vinegar and remove the pan from heat. According to an ancient tradition, you can now add the pine nuts and raisins. In a bowl, arrange a layer of sardines and and then place a layer of the onion mixture on top. Repeat until all the sardines and onion mixture has been used, then pour the remaining liquid over the top. Serve with plain bread. *Sardines in saòr* need to marinate for a few days in a cool and dry place before being served. If stored in the refrigerator, remember to remove them a few hours before serving.

Homemade
ice-cream

4 dl of fresh cream, 4 egg yolks,
4 tablespoons of sugar.

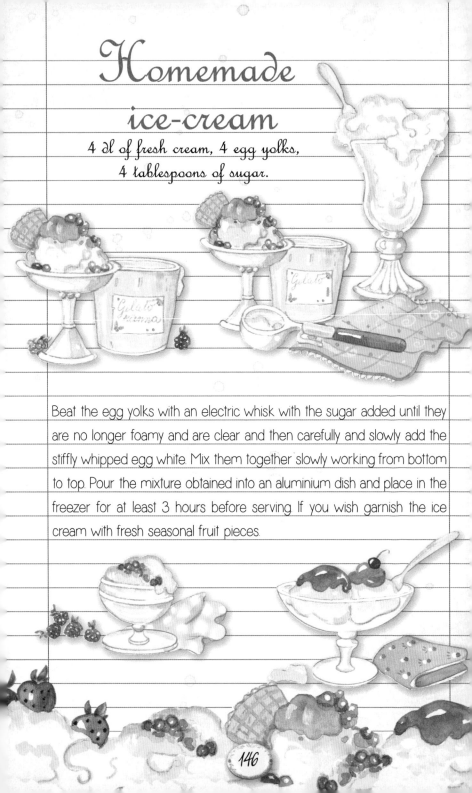

Beat the egg yolks with an electric whisk with the sugar added until they are no longer foamy and are clear and then carefully and slowly add the stiffly whipped egg white. Mix them together slowly working from bottom to top. Pour the mixture obtained into an aluminium dish and place in the freezer for at least 3 hours before serving. If you wish garnish the ice cream with fresh seasonal fruit pieces.

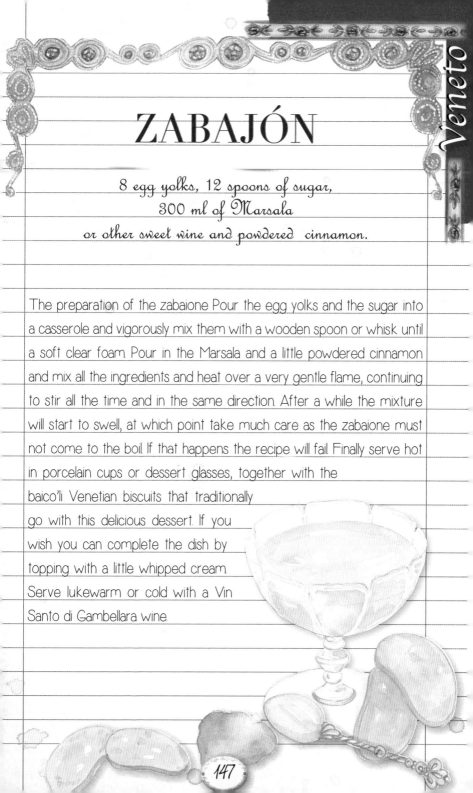

ZABAJÓN

8 egg yolks, 12 spoons of sugar,
300 ml of Marsala
or other sweet wine and powdered cinnamon.

The preparation of the zabaione Pour the egg yolks and the sugar into a casserole and vigorously mix them with a wooden spoon or whisk until a soft clear foam. Pour in the Marsala and a little powdered cinnamon and mix all the ingredients and heat over a very gentle flame, continuing to stir all the time and in the same direction. After a while the mixture will start to swell, at which point take much care as the zabaione must not come to the boil If that happens the recipe will fail. Finally serve hot in porcelain cups or dessert glasses, together with the baico'li Venetian biscuits that traditionally go with this delicious dessert. If you wish you can complete the dish by topping with a little whipped cream Serve lukewarm or cold with a Vin Santo di Gambellara wine.

4 live spider crabs (medium size),
2 lemons, 1 bunch chopped parsley
(optional), extra-virgin olive oil,
salt, freshly ground pepper.

With a brush, thoroughly clean the spider crabs, then tie their legs around the body with kitchen string, to avoid trouble in the next step. Plunge them in a pot of gently boiling water with half a lemon, salt and a few peppercorns. Let them cook for about twenty minutes, until the shells turn red. Let them cool in their cooking water, then drain, cut the strings and clean the shells. Female rock crabs carry eggs under the apron, so cut it open, remove the eggs and place them in a bowl. Carefully pull the abdomen away from the upper shell (you'll use the upper shell later on, so make sure you don't break it), discard the legs and all the cartilage. Pull out the coral and put it into a bowl. With your fingers, pull out all of the large chunks of meat and put them into the bowl with the coral; with the help of a sharpened stick, remove all the meat. Remove the creamy brownish guts and put them in the bowl with the eggs. With a nutcracker, break the legs and pull out the meat from the shell. Chop all the meat, mix it with the coral, and season with a pinch of salt and a marinade of pepper, lemon juice and a little olive oil. Mix everything together and then fill the shells with the crab mixture, sprinkling with a little chopped parsley (optional). Finally, mix the eggs with the brownish guts in their bowl and serve the mixture aside, for those who wish to combine it with the crab. Serve with Sauvignon Lison-Pramaggiore.

Granseola alla veneziana

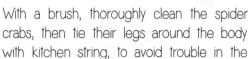

(Venetian-style spider crab)

300 g stale bread,
40 g butter, salt.

Cut the bread into small pieces, arrange them on the oven tray and toast in a pre-heated oven (100 °C), until the bread has taken a nice golden color. In an earthenware pot, bring to a boil 2 litres of lightly salted water. Add the toasted bread and simmer over low heat, stirring occasionally, until the bread is completely reduced to a mush. When the soup is ready, season with salt, add the butter and let it melt before serving. Some people prefer to use broth instead of water.

Panàda
(bread soup)

Orzét (barley soup)

200g pearl barley, 100 g bacon, 2 carrots,
2 medium potatoes, 1/2 stalk celery, 1 leek, salt.
To complete: 30 ml extra-virgin olive oil,
chives, 40 g grated Grana cheese from Trentino.

Orzét is a simple and tasty traditional barley soup from Trentino.
Peel the vegetables and cut them into tiny pieces. Sauté them in a pan over low heat, with the chopped bacon and barley. Pour the water, add a pinch of salt and cook the soup for 3 hours over very low heat. Season with salt, and serve the *orzét* with a drizzle of extra-virgin olive oil, a sprinkling of chives and some grated Grana cheese from Trentino on the side.

Canederli di magro
(bread balls, tipical simple fare from Dolomites)

300 g stale white bread, 50 g all-purpose flour,
1 small onion, 1 bunch parsley, 3 eggs,
30 g butter, 1 cup milk, salt.

Cut the bread into small pieces and place in an earthenware bowl. In a pan, sauté the finely chopped onion with butter. When browned, pour it over the bread along with the chopped parsley. In a separate bowl, beat the eggs with a little milk, season with salt and add the mixture to the other ingredients. Mix well, adding more milk if necessary - the bread should be well moistened but not soaked. Let the dough rest for at least 2 hours before cooking, so the flavours of all the ingredients will be well blended. In a saucepan, bring plenty of salted water to the boil. Meanwhile, prepare the dumplings: add to the bread mixture as much flour as necessary to achieve a not too soft nor too firm consistency. With wet hands, form balls of 4 cm in diameter; to make sure that the consistency of the dough is right, drop into the water a dumpling: if it becomes a mush, you should add more flour to the dough. When all the dumplings are ready, drop them in salted boiling water and cook over low heat for 10-15 minutes. Drain a dumpling and see if the inside is well cooked: when they are ready, pick up the dumplings with a slotted spoon, in order to drain the excess water. If you want to serve them in broth, place them in a bowl and pour hot low-fat broth over them. If you prefer, drain the *canederli* and season with melted butter and sage leaves. *Canederli* can be a great side dish to stewed or roasted meat or, alternatively, be served with a side dish of sauerkraut.

Strangolapreti

(spinach dumplings, literally 'priest-strangler)

800 g spinach, 100 g fresh ricotta, 2 stale white bread rolls,
2 eggs, 1 cup milk, 2 tablespoons flour, salt.
For the sauce: 80 g of butter, sage leaves,
40 g grated Parmesan.

Carefully trim the spinach, wash and boil in a little water; drain, squeeze well and chop. Cut the bread into small pieces, place in a bowl, moisten with the milk, stir and let stand. When the milk is completely absorbed, squeeze the bread to eliminate excess liquid and stir in the eggs, flour and a pinch of salt. Mix everything together, and then stir in the spinach and ricotta. Form dumplings about 3 cm in diameter and roll them in flour. In a saucepan, bring to a boil plenty of salted water. Gently plunge the *strangolapreti*, a few at a time, cooking them until they float up to the surface. Drain them with a slotted spoon and arrange in a baking dish, which will also work as a serving dish. Pour over the melted butter with the sage. Place the baking dish in a pre-heated oven for 5 minutes, in orders to evenly heat all *strangolapreti* Sprinkle with Parmesan cheese and serve.

Apple strudel

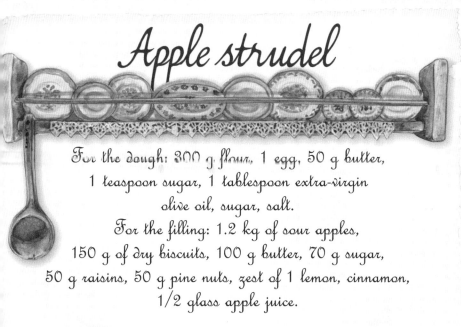

For the dough: 300 g flour, 1 egg, 50 g butter,
1 teaspoon sugar, 1 tablespoon extra-virgin
olive oil, sugar, salt.
For the filling: 1.2 kg of sour apples,
150 g of dry biscuits, 100 g butter, 70 g sugar,
50 g raisins, 50 g pine nuts, zest of 1 lemon, cinnamon,
1/2 glass apple juice.

Make a well with the flour and add a pinch of salt. Stir in the egg, sugar and softened butter. Gradually add about half a cup of warm water to give the dough the right consistency. Knead for 10 minutes, until the dough becomes smooth and elastic. Form a ball, grease with a little oil, cover with a cloth and leave to rest for half an hour. Meanwhile, rinse the raisins and leave to soak in a bowl of warm water. Peel the apples, remove the seeds, cut into slices and put them into a bowl. Add the sugar, a pinch of ground cinnamon, the pine nuts, raisins (drained and squeezed) and lemon zest. Mix well and leave to marinate in the fridge. On a floured tea cloth, roll out the dough with a rolling pin. Try to obtain a very thin pastry sheet, almost transparent, being careful not to break it. Brush it with melted butter and spread the two-thirds with the crumbled biscuits. Spread the apple mixture over on the pastry sheet. With the help of the tea cloth, roll the pastry up around the filling, and continue to roll until the filling is completely sealed in and the seam is on the bottom. Transfer the *strudel* to the baking tray (previously lined with parchment paper) and brush with the remaining melted butter. Bake in a pre-heated oven (200 °C) After about 30 minutes, brush the pastry with apple juice and leave to cook for a further 15-20 minutes. Serve hot, sprinkled with icing sugar.

Cjalcions
(sweet ravioli of Friuli)

For the dough: 500 g extra-fine flour, warm water and salt.
For the filling: 500 g boiled potatoes, 260 g herbs
(parsley, mint, marjoram, lemon balm, geranium, basil, thyme,
sage), 1 grated lemon zest, 1/2 teaspoon cinnamon,
1 tablespoon cocoa powder, 1 apple and 1 pear (grated),
50 g raisins, 2 crumbled dry biscuits, 100 g butter,
salt, smoked ricotta.

Boil or steam the potatoes, peel them and mash them. Sauté the herbs with the butter, then add them to the mashed potatoes; add the rest of the ingredients and knead thorougly. Prepare the dough with flour, warm water and salt, roll out and cut into discs (8 cm in diameter). Place a little heap of filling in the centre of each pasta disc, then fold over and seal the *cjalcions* (ravioli). Cook in plenty of boiling salted water and serve drizzled with melted butter (slightly browned), sprinkled with smoked ricotta and cinnamon.

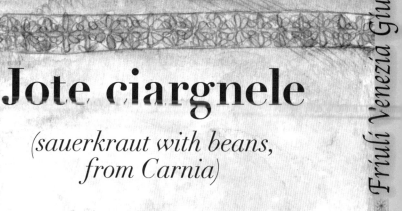

Jote ciargnele

(sauerkraut with beans, from Carnia)

300 g sauerkraut, 200 g dried borlotti beans from Carnia, 100 g pork with rind, 50 g bacon, 50 g pestât (lard with onion, garlic, parsley and chopped sage), extra-virgin olive oil, corn flour, extra-fine flour, salt

Soak the beans for 12 hours, drain them and boil in unsalted water. Add the rind, cut into small pieces.

In a pan, toast a spoonful of extra-fine flour with olive oil and add it to the beans. Sauté the *pestât*, when it's golden brown, add two handfuls of corn flour. Stir, and when the corn flour is evenly toasted add to the beans. Brown the bacon, add the sauerkraut, sauté for a few minutes and pour into the pot with the beans. Cook for a few minutes and serve hot.

Index of recipes

Acquacotta	55	Bucatini with sardines	
Agnolotti "del plin"	112	and fennel	6
Amaretti	106	Buccellato	107
Amaretti biscuits	23	Cacciucco alla livornese	82
Anchovies al verde	104	Caffè	36
Apple strudel	153	Canederli di magro	151
Arancini di riso	7	Cantucci	86
Arrosticini	51	Caprese salad	38
Artichokes alla giudia	63	Carasau bread with cheese	
Aubergine Caponata	9	and honey	16
Aubergine parmigiana	8	Casadinas	22
Baccalà alla vicentina	144	Cassata Siciliana	14
Baked cannelloni	91	Catalan-style lobster	20
Bean soup	65	Cheese and eggs	
Bistecca alla fiorentina	80	croquettes	46
Blanc manger	117	Cheeses	108
Bocconotti frentani	50	Chicken in potacchio	72
Bollito misto	142	Cjalcions	154
Bon brusà with lard	134	Crescentine nelle tigelle	87
Bonet	118	Crostoni	
Bresaola, arugula		with Tuscan Kale	74
and Parmesan	120	Crumiri	117
Brò brusà with oil	134	Erbazzone	88
Brodetto alla fanese	68	Fagioli all'uccelletto	83
Bruschetta	52	Fegato alla veneziana	143
Bucatini alla matriciana	58	Finanziera	115

Focaccia di Recco	101	Panzanella	73
Fonduta valdostana	119	Pappa col pomodoro	25
Fried onion rings	26	Pappardelle	
Fritto misto,		with chicken livers	135
Piedmont style	114	Pappardelle	
Granseola		with wild boar	77
alla veneziana	148	Pasqualina (Easter) pie	100
Hazelnut cake	116	Passatelli in hot meat stock	94
Home-made Pasta	92	Pasta e fagioli	134
Homemade bread	32	Pastiera napoletana	43
Homemade ice-cream	146	Pearà sauce	141
Jote ciargnele	155	Pesto alla Genovese	102
La mugnaia	49	Piadina romagnola	89
La sbrisolona	128	Pike with sauce	
Lamb ribs alla calabrese	27	and polenta	131
Maccheroni alla chitarra		Pizza Margherita	39
with meat sauce	48	Pizzoccheri	
Malloreddus		della Valtellina	122
"alla campidanese"	18	Polenta	133
Meat sauce		Porcheddu carriaxiu	19
with aromatic vinegar	90	Pork medallions	
Milanese saffron risotto	124	with 'nduja	29
Milanese veal cutlet	127	Potato croquettes	53
Mostaccioli	15	Potato gnocchi	140
Mostarda di Cremona	121	Potato tortelli	79
Mozzarelle in carrozza	35	Prosciutto and melon	97
Mussels au gratin	31	Pumpkin cappellacci	96
None of the pig		Puntarelle with anchovies	62
in wasted!	84	Rabbit "alla cacciatora"	28
Octopus		Rabbit in potacchio	72
and potatoes salad	105	Ravioli della Val Pusteria	78
Olive all'ascolana	67	Ribollita	75
Orecchiette alla barese	34	Rigatoni alla norcina	64
Orecchiette		Risotto al nero di seppia	139
with broccoli rabe	34	Risotto alla pilòta	125
Orzét	150	Risotto with Amarone	137
Ossibuchi with peas	127	Risotto with asparagus	138
Panàda	149	Risotto	
Panettone	129	with veal marrow	111

Roast kid with potatoes 11
Roast spring lamb 60
Rum Babà 42
Sagne a pezze
 with cicerchie 47
Saltimbocca alla romana 61
Sarde in saòr 145
Sardines a beccafico 12
Sardinian-style
 sea bream 21
Sausage
 and shallot frittata 66
Sebada 24
Sicilian cannoli 13
Spaghetti alla carbonara 57
Spaghetti alla carrettiera 59
Spaghetti alla marinara 40
Spaghetti alla Norma 5
Spaghetti cacio
 and pepper 56
Spaghetti with bottarga 17
Spaghetti with clams 41
Spaghetti with garlic,
 olive oil
 and chili pepper 76
Strangolapreti 152
Strozzapreti
 alla boscaiola 95
Stuffed artichokes
 "alla messinese" 10

Stuffed courgettes 97
Stuffed deep-fried
 courgette flowers 126
Supplì alla romana 54
Swordfish "a ghiotta" 30
Tagliatelle, pappardelle
 and tagliolini 93
Tajarin 113
Tarallini 33
The different loaves
 and rolls 70
The fabulous story
 of the three sisters
 and their special
 Polenta 132
The shapes
 of pasta from "A" to "Z" 44
Tiramisù 98
Torta delle rose 130
Trenette with Genovese
 pesto sauce 103
Trippa alla fiorentina 81
Trofie
 with Genovese pesto 103
Turtéi d' süca 123
Valeggio-style tortellini 136
Vincisgrassi 69
Vitello tonnato 110
Zabajón 147
Zuppa inglese (trifle) 99

Finito di stampare nel mesi di settembre
presso Grafiche Busti srl - Colognola ai Colli - VR